W9-BQM-413

THE EAST-CENTRAL
EUROPEAN REGION

THE EAST-CENTRAL
EUROPEAN REGION

An Historical Outline

George H. Hodos

 PRAEGER

Westport, Connecticut
London

147159

Library of Congress Cataloging-in-Publication Data

Hodos, George H.
     The East-Central European region : an historical outline
  / George H. Hodos.
        p.   cm.
     Includes bibliographical references and index.
     ISBN 0–275–95497–8 (alk. paper)
     1. Europe, Eastern—History.   2. Europe, Central—History.
  I. Title.
  DJK38.H63   1999
  943'.0009717—dc21   99–20924

British Library Cataloguing in Publication Data is available.

Library of Congress Catalog Card Number: 99–20924
ISBN: 0–275–95497–8

First published in 1999

Praeger Publishers, 88 Post Road West, Westport, CT 06881
An imprint of Greenwood Publishing Group, Inc.
www.praeger.com

Printed in the United States of America

The paper used in this book complies with the
Permanent Paper Standard issued by the National
Information Standards Organization (Z39.48–1984).

10 9 8 7 6 5 4 3 2 1

Contents

Preface

I am offering the reader a rather small book about a very large subject, a thousand-year-long history of the East-Central European region. The idea was borne from long reflections on my short life connected to this small unhappy part of the world. The impulse for my previous book about postwar Stalinist terror (*Show Trials*, Praeger, 1987) came from the bitter five years spent in Hungarian prisons on concocted political charges. How and why could this have happened, I asked myself. How and why could it have happened that my father, my grandmother, all my aunts, uncles, and cousins perished in the Holocaust? How could I have believed, in October 1956, that the dream of my youth, a democratic socialism, could be made possible? Why was this belief crushed in November by Soviet armed intervention that led to my immigration to the West? Was all that only the doing of Hitler and Stalin, or do I have to dig much deeper?

The search for answers led me further and further back in the history of East-Central Europe and ultimately to writing this book. The roots of German fascism and Stalinist communism reach back to the fifteenth century—to refeudalization of Prussia and the introduction of state serfdom in Muscovy. The shattered socialist ideal has its early counterpart in the suppression of a democratic dream in the 1848 Hungarian revolution by the Russian army. The especially brutal character of a long chain of tragedies, which time and again blocked the way to a better society, was not the fate of Hungary alone, it was the historically developed destiny of the entire East-Central European region. To find answers to the present, one has to research the past.

This book is necessarily only a concise outline of the complex history of the region from cradle to grave. The past cannot fully explain the present, much less predict the future, but it can set limits to change and project its general direction. That is why the outline ends with a mixture of hope and resignation. I wish the future would confirm the hope and disprove the resignation.

Acknowledgments

My deepest thanks go to Professor Ivan T. Berend, director of the Center for European and Russian Studies, at the University of California, Los Angeles (UCLA). This book could not have been written without his friendship, encouragement, and comments. Many of my chapters are based on his insights, as well as the wealth of facts and figures in his works.

My thanks go also to Kati Radics, West European bibliographer at the UCLA Research Library. Forgiving my technical ignorance, she helped to find, in the mysterious labyrinth of computerized directories, many useful source publications.

I want also to express my gratitude to the directors and colleagues at the Institutes of Historical Science and of Political History in Budapest, Hungary, as well as at the Center for Historical Research in Potsdam, Germany, for their advice and the use of their research libraries.

I am sincerely thankful for the interest and care that this book has received from Heather R. Staines, history editor at Praeger, publisher of my previous work, for her kind suggestions and review and for her patience with my occasionally slow progress.

Last, I owe a debt of gratitude to my wife Judy and my family, whose confidence helped me overcome periods of discouragement in finishing the seemingly endless task of a thousand-year-long-history of a region that also formed my personal history.

1

Birth of the Western Region

THE ENGLISH AND THE FRENCH MODEL

The history of Europe began in the West, with the establishment of the Frankish-Carolingian Empire in the ninth century. Its frontiers formed the demarcation line beyond which "Europe" was nothing more than a geographic notion. East of the empire stretched "eastern Europe," at the time a concept without any content, a vast territory slowly filled with nomadic tribes that poured in from Asia during the centuries of the Great Migration of such peoples as Bulghars and Avars, Khazars and Magyars, or the Slavs branching out radiating east, west, and south from their original center between the Vistula and the Dnieper. In the south, Carolingian Europe was blocked by the Byzantine Empire based in Asia Minor, in the southwest corner by the Arab conquests reaching from North Africa deep into the Iberian Peninsula.

The Carolingian Empire gave birth not only to Europe, but also to its specific structure, western feudalism, the social foundation on which the evolving West was built, until capitalism replaced it. The western model of feudalism was shaped by an organic synthesis of late antique Roman-Christian and barbarian-German elements. It was made possible by the disintegration of the Roman Empire and, with it, the collapse of political sovereignty, the state, and all the traditional juridical, social cohesive forces. The only power surviving the chaos was the Catholic Church, but in the ninth century, even it abandoned any pretention of "caesaro-papism."

Western feudalism developed into a structure of customary, personal, mutually secured obligations and rights, a system of small circles of "freedoms" balancing each other—king, church, lord, vassal, serf—thus preventing the concentration of power or a unilateral submission. This structure helped to achieve a separation of state and society, spiritual and secular, ideological and political spheres. It was a structure that carried in its feudal integument the seeds for the evolution of later freedoms: the emancipation of society, the coming of national states, Renaissance and Reformation, the Social Contract, popular sovereignty, and democracy of a much later period.

In the chaotic world of the dissolution of state power, the emerging western feudalism provided protection and power prestige with its system of specific personal, private contracts. All the social elements were integrated into it, not side by side, or under the state, but substituting it. This contractual character established the customary duties and obligations of the lord and the vassal, an unequal contract between the powerful and the weak; nevertheless it carried in it the later possibility to be used from the bottom up, a future promise of "freedom" for the peasants, however limited and conditional.

Another characteristic of the western feudal model was its retention of human dignity. Even within their subordination, vassals did not approach the lord with handkiss, nor did they go down on their knees to kiss the hem of his dress, as was the custom everywhere else at that time. In the West, the vassal approached the lord with head erect, bent his knee, lord and peasant touched each other's palms, and exchanged kisses to seal their relation.

Though only symbols, these aspects nonetheless characterize the unique content of western feudalism. The formal ceremony that grew into feudal homage and the oath of fealty reveals the honorable position of the vassal and his pride in the idea that faith and service should be due on both sides in equal measure.

The symbols also had relevant consequences: every western peasant uprising justified its revolt with the landlord's breach of contract and demanded its right to "freedom." Only western feudalism organically merged knightly honor and vassal fidelity. Human dignity, as a constitutive element of political relations, is not a heritage of antiquity, but of western feudalism.

Of utmost importance is the emergence of autonomous cities with their specific "liberties" and the development of an urban economy during three centuries. It became the motor and center of a rapid growth of western feudalism, a growth that collided with the limits of the structure around the year 1300. The ensuing severe crisis of the agrarian and monetary system was accompanied by famines, widespread death, drastic depopulation and decay of villages, knightly banditism, and anarchy.

It was the urban economy that regenerated first, by locating new markets, mainly in east-central Europe where it found a source to satisfy the growing need for precious metals in the medieval cities. The impetus given by a newly expanding urban economy became a decisive factor in overcoming the general crisis and helped to bring about significant changes in the feudal structures.

The main result was the radical loosening of the obligations of the serfs. By the end of the Middle Ages, money, rent, and tenantship became the dominant regulatory principle of the relationship between lord and peasant. At the same time, the monarchies took advantage of the prospering cities and the exhausted nobility. The monarchs gained the upper hand in the horizontally divided society and changed not only the power relations, but also the geographical limits of the region. The strengthened monarchies started a vast new expansion of the West which led, through discovery and colonization, to establish the foundations of the world economy of modern times and, a century later, to the emergence of absolutism.

The vastly expanded world market became the main stimulus in developing new forms of production; it undermined the economic basis of serfdom, despite the desperate attempts by the absolute monarchs to use their control of the state to maintain the essentials of their feudal power. The collapse of western feudalism, however, was inevitable. The breakthrough occurred in England with the convocation of the Long Parliament in 1640, the two civil wars, and the beheading of King Charles in 1649. On the rapidly crumbling ruins of feudal institutions, a new society was emerging, led by a strong bourgeoisie. The road was now open for the original accumulation of capital, which exploded in the Industrial Revolution in the mid–eighteenth century.

The pioneer role of England in the economic transformation was taken over in the political field by France just a few decades later with the Great Revolution. The two revolutions swept away the remnants of feudalism and triggered the triumph of capitalism and democracy in the western region of Europe.

* * *

A closer look at the history of England and France illustrates the two classical methods, one slow and organic, the other a sudden violent explosion. Both transformed the feudal, ecclesialist order in a secular capitalist society and led, eventually, to democracy in the western region.

From the fourteenth century onward, commerce became increasingly important in both the towns and the countryside of England. By the late Middle Ages, England had become the largest source of wool with its markets on the continent, particularly in Italy and in the Low Countries. A century later, the Wars of the Roses brought tremendous bloodletting to the ruling landed aristocracy and enabled the Tudor dynasty to consolidate royal power. To regain lost terrain, the feudal nobility, impressed by the greatly enriched wool traders in the towns, began to develop a commercial outlook. Land that until then had had mainly military and social significance, gained an increasingly economic value. Command of money became more important than the command of men. This change marked the transition from the medieval conception of land as the basis of political functions and obligations to the viewing of it as an income-yielding investment. Landholding was gradually commercialized, to be treated as something that could be bought and sold, an adaptation of the landed aristocracy to the new situation created by the enriched commercial class.

Among the most important structural developments in sixteenth-century agriculture was the beginning of the "enclosures," the encroachment of the landlords or their big tenant farmers upon the land, over which the manorial population had common rights or which lay on the open arable fields free to be used by everybody. Peasants were deprived of those rights, and land started to be used at the discretion of its holder for commercial purposes. The feudal seigneur was transformed into a businessman exploiting the material resources of the estate, now mainly changed from grain to wool, with an eye to profit and efficiency. The yeomen, the upper ranks of the peasantry, followed suit and became one of the chief forces behind peasant enclosures, gradually sloughing off their remaining feudal obligations. Landlords and yeomen were the main victors in promoting agrarian capitalism, while the main victims of progress were the ordinary peasants, driven off the land. The plowed strips and commons were turned into pastures.

Landlords and the gentry, the large middle nobility between the titled aristocrats and the yeomanry, became the leading force of opposition against the royal power and its policy to attempt the preservation of the old order. They formed all sorts of personal and business connections with the upper strata of wealthy urban bourgeoisie, an alliance that further promoted a commercial and capitalist agriculture in the countryside. It led to the formation of a united coherent opposition against a Crown unable to build an effective administration and legal machinery to stem the progress steadily advancing in the seventeenth century.

The tensions erupted in civil war. It swept away royal absolutism and, with it, the main barrier to the enclosing landlords, but it did not achieve a bourgeoisie revolution. The landed upper classes remained in firm control. The aristocratic order survived, but in a new form with money more than birth as its basis. The Parliament—the roots of which reach back to the fourteenth century—became the instrument of the landed capitalists and their allies in the towns; it was their interests that the state now pursued. While the original impulse toward capitalism had come from the towns far back in the Middle Ages, it proceeded in the countryside as well as in the cities. It brought the triumph of the capitalist principle—production for profit rather than for use—and led ultimately to the triumph of parliamentary democracy. With the beheading of Charles I, the divine support of royal authority was broken; Charles's fate was a reminder for the future, no subsequent English king tried to revive royal absolutism.

The outcome of the civil war greatly strengthened the position of the landed upper classes. The next hundred years were the golden age of the big estates, an age of improvement in agricultural techniques such as the increased use of fertilizer, new crops, and crop rotation. The landlords' contribution to capitalist farming was mainly legal and political. They lacked serfs and let out the land to big tenant farmers who came up with the working capital, hired the work force, and paid rent to the estate holder.

The weakening of royal power eliminated the king as the last protection of the peasants against the encroachment of the aristocratic landlords. The rapid expansion of the enclosures dealt a final blow that destroyed the whole structure of English peasant society embodied in the traditional village. Now its accelerated progress was controlled by the Parliament, which itself was dominated by the landed upper classes. Peasant property and common fields were swallowed up by a legal, but nonetheless ruthless process that led to a concentration of the land in fewer hands. The enclosures broke up some 6 million acres of common fields and transformed them into the private properties of the landlords. By the mid–nineteenth century, some four thousand mostly commercially managed large estates owned close to half of the total land, cultivated by a quarter of a million mostly middle-sized farmers who employed one and a quarter million hired laborers. Peasants made landless and semi-landless farm laborers were the victims of the enclosures, and the Poor Laws rendered the life of the pauperized masses so intolerable as to force them to migrate to any jobs that the industrializing city offered.

By the 1850s, the peasantry had been eliminated as a factor in British political life. The landlords acted as an advance guard for industrial capitalism, and modernization could now proceed without the huge reservoir of conservative and reactionary forces that existed in France and in Germany. The "surplus" peasants became a reserve army to feed industry with cheap manpower. Rural capitalism provided a mechanism for the accumulation of capital in the industrial sectors of the economy.

Vast overseas expansion also had a decisive influence on the transformation. The foreign policy of the British government became subordinated to the economy and its wars were aimed at the interests of trade and commerce. Britain gained a factual world monopoly in overseas colonies, exclusive control of the seas, and eliminated all competitors.

While commerce expanded manyfold, industry progressed only slowly. It retained its basic preindustrial structures and technologies and its rural character. The change came at the beginning of the eighteenth century and exploded in its last quarter in the Industrial Revolution. It was cotton that initiated the surge and brought about a mechanized factory system that produced in such vast quantities at diminishing costs as to no longer be dependent on existing demand, but to create its own market.

Colonial trade created the cotton industry. The raw material came from the overseas colonies and semicolonies. Within fifty years, the export markets of Europe, South America, Africa, and Asia became practical monopolies of the rapidly mechanized and astronomically growing British cotton industry. The wealth, the rapid capital accumulation created by the cotton industry, was invested in railway building, which became the second big impulse for the pioneering Industrial Revolution. In 1830, there were only a few dozen miles of railways in all of Europe. Twenty years later, the number surged to 23,500 miles, most built in large part with British capital, iron, machines, and know-how. The immense needs of the railways for iron, steel and coal, for heavy machinery and capital investment provided the massive demand that was necessary to transform the capital-goods industry as profoundly as the cotton industry. Both created the takeoff for modern industrial capitalism, and they also changed the social character of British democracy from agrarian-commercial to bourgeois.

Cotton and railways gave the main stimuli that rapidly involved all British industry, and in its wake, industrialization, the capitalist development of western Europe followed. Britain became the "workshop of the modern world"; its pioneering role transformed the western continent and shook off the feudal shackles of the productive power of human society.

The French political revolution changed the western world as deeply as the English industrial one, though from the late Middle Ages onward, it took a different road to democracy. While in England, the nobility gained a substantial independence from the Crown, the French aristocracy became a decorative appendage of the absolute monarch. In England, the landed upper classes adopted a capitalist agriculture; in France they went on to live from feudal dues extracted from the peasants. Commerce and manufacturing with a strong economic base lagged far behind. Prejudice against trying to make money from farming was extremely influential among the aristocracy and the court nobility. Any noble man who engaged in a "demeaning occupation," such as operating a retail shop to sell grain, or working on more than a small portion of his land, lost his noble status. Royal absolutism wanted a prosperous nobility as a decorative adjunct to the Crown and to help keep the people in their "proper place," but it did not want them to establish an independent economic base to challenge royal power. The English development resulted in the destruction of the peasants, the French in the destruction of the aristocracy.

The incipient urban bourgeoisie split in the seventeenth and eighteenth centuries. Part of it became heavily dependent on the king, on royal favors and regulations. The manufacturers and traders among them oriented their production toward arms and luxuries for a restricted clientele. The monarchy absorbed many into landed aristocracy and made them defenders of noble privileges. The other part among the growing commercial class started, by the beginning of the eighteenth century, to demand the loosening of the feudal fetters, free competition, and property rights. Though still within the prevailing system, their learned members began to formulate the outlines of an order based on the natural right of freedom and egality.

A substantial part of the peasants had become personally free and owners of the lord's property. Noble and clerical estates covered only one-fourth of the land. The majority of the peasantry was landless or worked on insufficient holdings to make an adequate living for themselves and their families. Feudal dues, tithes, and taxes took a rising portion of their income, and inflation reduced the value of the remainder. In times of bad harvest, famine prices ruled; that is what happened in the years preceding the revolution when real hunger, together with general land hunger, made Europe's relatively most prosperous peasantry a major force for revolt and change.

The rising social tensions between the bourgeoisie and peasant demands and the immobility of royal absolutism did not lead immediately to an open rebellion. The terrain was prepared by the near-financial bankruptcy of the monarchy, due to a grossly obsolete administration and fiscal structure, and was triggered by France's costly involvement in the American War of Independence.

The Revolution was introduced by the ensuing impoverishment of the aristocracy. The response of the nobility was twofold. It attempted to recapture the state from the king, refused to pay without the extension of its privileges, and tried to revive the long-buried feudal assembly as a counterweight to absolute monarchy. The other answer was to extract increased feudal dues from the peasants. The landlords lacked the capitalistic spirit of their English counterparts, and squeezing out of "their" peasants a much larger share of the crop was the only way they knew how to keep a luxurious standard of living and to feed the restless townspeople.

The seigneurial reaction to the crisis radicalized the peasants as well as the bourgeoisie. The rich peasants resented the higher feudal dues enforced by the aristocrats, and they also turned against the king who supported the encroachment of the landlords upon their holdings. The poor and landless peasants turned against both the nobility and the king. Demands rose among their ranks to abolish all dues, whether in kind or in cash.

The commercial bourgeoisie, increasingly enriched by the rapid development of foreign trade and colonialism, became radicalized by the liberal ideas of the philosophers and by the demands of the physiocrat economists for free enterprise and trade, a rational fiscal and administrative policy. The famous Declaration of the Rights of Man was a manifesto against the hierarchical order of noble privilege, however, not in favor of a democratic society or a republic. The liberal bourgeois of 1789 was a believer in constitutionalism, a secular state with civil liberties and guarantees for private enterprise, a government by taxpayers and property owners, with a ruler no longer the monarch by the grace of God, but the King of the French and the Nation as the source of all sovereignty.

Bad harvests made the crisis more acute, which hurt the peasantry. The market for traders and manufacturers was reduced and caused a depression in the towns and cities with rising unemployment for the urban poor, the *sans-culottes* whose work ceased and whose cost of living soared. The country poor became desperate and restless with riots and banditry. At the time of major convulsion, reform turned into the idea of liberation from noble society and royal oppression; a riotous people stood behind the revolting Third Estate, a fictional entity including all who were neither noble nor clergy, but who in fact were dominated by the middle class.

Counterrevolution changed a potential mass rising into an actual one. It was the concentration of troops around the capital that mobilized the Paris masses, already hungry and militant, and led to the capture of the Bastille. The fall of this state prison, symbolizing royal authority, ratified the fall of the old order and started the Revolution.

French society could not generate a parliament of capitalist-minded landlords with bourgeois overtones, as had evolved in England, without a political revolution. Royal absolutism used the nobility as the crown jewel of its court, and the aristocracy remained opposed to liberal democracy to the end. It adapted to the gradual intrusion of capitalism by feudal means, by increasing the pressure on the peasants. The alliance of the nobility and part of the upcoming urban middle class was achieved by the monarch who "bought" the upper ranks of the bourgeoisie and, with it, "feudalized" them rather than the other way around, as in England.

The revolutionary destruction of the *ancien regime* did not start as a bourgeois revolution since royal absolutism had prevented its growing strong enough. Instead, the upper ranks of the bourgeoisie rose to power on the backs of the radical urban poor at the moment when the crisis of the monarchy neared collapse. These radical forces prevented the Revolution from stopping at the establishment of a secular constitutional monarchy. The peasant masses took advantage of the situation and abolished feudalism, one of the main achievements of the Revolution.

For a time, rural and urban radicalism pushed the Revolution forward to its most radical phases. But the need to get food to the poorer townsmen and to the revolutionary army collided with the interests of the upper ranks in the peasantry. It removed the popular support of the Jacobin Republic and brought the radical revolution to a halt. The *sans-culottes* made the bourgeois revolution; the peasants determined just how far it could go.

The Revolution remained, in a sense, unfinished. A large class of small and middle peasants, small craftsmen and shopkeepers were among the main victors who have dominated the country's life ever since. The capitalist part of the French economy became a superstructure erected on the immovable base of peasantry and petty bourgeoisie. Deep in the nineteenth—even in the twentieth—century, standardized cheap goods, which made the fortunes of progressive industrialists elsewhere, lacked a sufficiently large and expanding market. Significant segments of French industrialists made luxury goods and not goods for mass consumption; financiers promoted foreign rather than home industries. The capitalist transformation was not completed in the English way, with the destruction of the peasantry. The progress of industrialization was slowed down and delayed for a long time the establishment of a full-blown democracy.

The British industrial and the French political revolutions deeply influenced the history of the East-Central European region, the main subject of this book. It was England's answer to the structural crisis of western feudalism in the late Middle Ages and the threat of feudal disintegration that prompted the east-central European nobility to seek the opposite answer, the strengthening of feudalism with the Second Serfdom, that broke away from the West and created a new region.

More direct was the influence of the French Revolution. Its ideals of liberty and equality, the identification of the "people" instead of the nobility with the nation, found deep resonance in all the countries of the region. They tried to imitate the revolutionary French road out of backwardness—out of a Middle Age prolonged into the nineteenth century. That this example had been turned into aborted and distorted "revolutions from above" had its roots, as we shall see, 350 years ago when, contrary to the English and the French roads, in a fateful retreat to the past, they halted progress for centuries to come.

2

The Eastern Region

FROM ITS BIRTH TO THE BOLSHEVIK REVOLUTION

The direct influence of the eastern region on the history of East-Central Europe has been negligible, except for the annexation of portions of partitioned Poland and the short Russian occupation of Moldavia and Walachia in the formative years of Rumania.

In contrast to East-Central Europe, the birth of the eastern region did not evolve by a rupture with the West (of which it never had been a part). It did not develop from western structures built on the ruins of the collapsed Roman Empire. The eastern region became a closed society, cutting itself off from western, as well as East-Central regions of Europe. Even the apparent similarity of the Second Serfdom with that in the latter region had a much different social and historical background and contained many different structures.

We deal with this region mainly to contrast it with the West and with our focal point, East-Central Europe. We do not follow its metamorphosis into the Soviet system, however; we will return to it in a much later period and in a much different connection, the

Soviet incorporation of the East-Central area into the Stalinized Eastern region.

The social structure of the Eastern region—roughly equivalent to the Russian Empire—followed a different path, right from its beginnings in the formative centuries of historical Europe. Its roots reach back to the sixth century, when Slavic tribes settled on the Russian plains and later established the semistate of Rus, with Kiev at its center. Rus survived the conquest of the nomadic Varangians from the north and the Khazars from the southeast and adopted Christianity in its Byzantine form in the year 988. However, by the twelfth century, Rus had disintegrated into dozens of small principalities, which became easy prey of the Mongol invasion and were absorbed into the Khanate of the Golden Horde. It was under the Mongols that the principality of Moscow asserted its position as nucleus of the future Russia.

Around A.D. 800, a kind of protofeudalism began to emerge, a mixture of southern Byzantine, northern nomadic-barbarian, and far eastern Mongol influences, and evolved into a specific eastern form of feudalism: state-serfdom.

In sharp contrast to the western model with its horizontal structure, a vertical hierarchy developed. At the top were the princes and the dukes. On the next rung came their councillors, the boyars whose power was purely local and who lacked any hereditary rights, thus preventing the formation of a settled aristocratic class for centuries. Below the boyars was the scattered class of feudal landlords. The bottom was formed by three layers of a heterogenous peasantry: the free peasants, breaking the new soil of the vast expanding territory of the Russian plains; then the peasant majority, living in different forms of feudal dependence; and below them all, the peasant serfs, retaining many archaic characteristics of slavery. Even the church was subordinate to the prince. The city dwellers along the main trading routes did not attain the autonomous status of their burgher counterparts in the western feudal model and were dominated by the boyars. While in the West, feudalism developed and changed organically due to the spontaneous forces of its inner structure, in the East adjustments to developing serfdom were mainly introduced from above.

Parallel to the evolution of feudalism was a steady expansion of Muscovy. At the very end of the fifteenth century, it gained its independence from the disintegrating Mongol Empire. In the next century, it conquered the Khanates of Kazan and Astrakhan, detached the southern Ukraine from the Kingdom of Poland, and extended its rule over Siberia. With it, the boundaries of the Eastern European region, once a mere geographic notion, were nearly complete.

The great crisis of feudalism reached Russia in the seventeenth century with similar symptoms as were described in the western region: famines, Black Death, depopulation, decay of villages, banditry, and political anarchy. The answer to this general crisis was, however, very different. While western feudalism overcame the crisis by loosening serfdom, in the east, to the contrary, feudal bonds were tightened and frozen.

The widespread death and the expansion of Russia caused a mass flight of peasants to the newly conquered territories and left vast areas of Muscovy abandoned. The ensuing labor shortage led to a severe decline in demesne cultivation and in labor services. This was the basis of the famous Code of 1649, issued by Prince Ivan III. It established the Second Serfdom and extended with it the eastern type of feudalism for two more centuries. The code granted the landlords unlimited rights to "their" peasants, including the right to bring back fugitives and bind them to their estates. The mobility of the serfs was abolished; the landowner could sell "his" serfs, exchange them, punish them, split up families and, in general, treat them as chattel. The formerly free peasants colonizing the new territories became state serfs.

The Second Serfdom became the predominant structure of the Russian feudal system. It strengthened not only the feudal economy, but also the absolute power of the prince, Ivan III, who gave himself, for the first time, the title "Sovereign of All Russia," symbol of the emerging eastern absolutism that predated its western counterpart by one hundred years. While in the West, absolutism remained a historical episode on the way to capitalism, in the eastern model, autocratic Tsarist absolutism became the structure itself and served for centuries as a framework for every change. It developed into a tacit contract between the Tsar-dominated state and the nobility: in exchange for a state guarantee to deprive the peasantry of all rights and to secure the feudal socage, the nobility abdicated its role in the state structure.

In western, as in eastern absolutism, the nobility was the foundation of the bureaucracy and the military. In the West, the feudal state "bought" a part of the nobility by selling administrative-political and military positions and neutralized the other part by securing its privileges. In the eastern absolutistic model, already in the fifteenth century, a nobility of office was created whose position in the state was entirely dependent on the ruler. The landlord held his land only as long as he served the Tsar. Peter the Great developed this system further by classifying all ranks in the military and bureaucracy into fourteen grades, thus creating a kind of "nationalized" unified service nobility.

Those reforms were linked with a further intensification of the rule over the peasants. A poll tax was imposed; forced labor introduced in the new state-owned mines, factories, ironworks, and construction; and an internal passport system obliged every serf to secure his owner's written permission to leave his village, a system that lasted until the Bolshevik Revolution.

In the eastern model of feudalism, all strata of society became subjects of the Tsarist absolutism. The Orthodox Church enjoyed authority merely as deputies of the state. In the western model, absolute monarchies' mercantilism became the breeding ground of capitalism, Russian mercantilism evolved into an extension of Tsarist monopoly over commerce and manufacture; it secured the dominant role of the state in foreign trade, as well as in all branches of key industries, especially those with military importance. In contrast to the western model, where economic growth helped the rise of a bourgeoisie, in Russia it was the state that got further strengthened. Contrary to the role of the eastern cities, Russian cities did not succeed in separating themselves from agriculture. They served as commercial, administrative, and military centers of the absolute state and remained centers of consumption, not production.

The divergence in the western and eastern feudal absolutistic structures became even more pronounced in the following centuries. To be competitive, Peter the Great and his successors were compelled to open the window to Europe and give up their separate "world economy." The Russian Empire had to become part of the European economy and civilization, but at the same time, had to secure the all-mighty autocracy. Enlightenment became a state affair by "civilizing" its subjects in such a way that their character as subjects was fully preserved.

The reforms of Peter the Great were not so much efforts to Europeanize Russia, but rather a logical completion of a specific, separate East European model. They brought to perfection the limited possibilities of movements in a distinct "nationalized" region, movements directed exclusively from above within an essentially immobile social-political structure. In the West, as in the East, absolutism hammered out the nation-state. In the West, however, the free sovereign nation seized control over the state, while in the East, the social frame of the Russian nation remained subordinate to the freedom of Tsarist autocracy.

In the period when the English and the French revolutions triggered a dramatic, explosive change from feudalism to capitalism and democracy, in Tsarist Russia, the transition got stuck midway. Industrialization was also a function of the state and depended on it. The state was the market for the goods produced; it supplied capital and even labor by forcing state serfs into factories. Arising late, industry did not repeat the western development, but adapted its latest achievements to its own backwardness. This led to a rapidly heightened tension between an advanced superstructure of a state-dependent, pseudocapitalist industrial-commercial growth and an immobile base of autocratic state feudalism. In agriculture, similar tensions arose between a stationary agricultural yield and the state monopoly's requirement for an increased grain export, between the feudal landlords' requirement for capital and for a free, skilled, productive supply of labor, and the rigid feudal structure.

The Tsar tried to solve these tensions with the Ukaz of 1861, which abolished serfdom from above. The serf became a free citizen, free to marry, to own property, and who could no longer be bought and sold. However, the abolition of serfdom was done in sharp contrast to the western model. Feudalism was not undermined from below by the growing strength of a bourgeoisie, but essentially abolished in agreement between the Tsar and the feudal landowners who sought free development of their estates. In Russia, serfdom was abolished by preserving most of the prerogatives of the nobility and, above all, autocratic absolutism.

However, the necessity of a radical structural change was unavoidable. A belated, distorted East European semicapitalism in an overwhelmingly agricultural, semifeudal country with a fast-growing heavy industry, under control of the state and of foreign capital, was confronted with the demands of a developing, but still insignificant middle class, the masses of impoverished, land-hungry peasantry, and a suddenly increased, highly concentrated working class. The conflicting interests reached the crisis point in 1905 in the failed workers' revolution and peasant uprising. Twelve years later, it was the turn of the Bolsheviks. Their revolution destroyed the Tsarist, feudal, and nascent bourgeois structures and introduced an autocratic dictatorship to bring the region into the twentieth century.

3

The East-Central Region

BETWEEN WEST AND EAST

Central Europe was born as a child of the West, who later married the East. It appeared on the political map of Europe around the year 1000. Within a few decades, the fluid contours of tribal settlements stabilized into states: Slavic tribes in the north united in 963 into the Principality of Poland; Magyar clans from Asia penetrated at the very end of the ninth century into the Carpathian Basin and established the principality of Hungary. To the west, the Czech-Bohemian Kingdom of Moravia was first destroyed by the Magyar invasion, then occupied by Germany. To the south, the Hungarians annexed to their kingdom the Slavic Croatia.

Together, with the formation and stabilization of the political map of Central Europe, went the Christianization of the region: Poland in 966, Hungary in 1000, the German-annexed Moravia in 929, and the Hungarian-annexed Croatia in 1091.

Stabilization and Christianization also meant the eastward expansion of the western region from its core, the Kingdoms of France, Germany, and Italy, successors of the divided Carolingian Empire. Central Europe became the periphery of the western region. The original Carolingian demarcation line moved some 500 miles to the east, to run from the western border of Kiev-Rus and the Carpathian Mountains in a nearly straight line to the south, until it reached the frontiers of the Byzantine Empire. The new demarcation line also divided, since the Great Schism in 1054, western and eastern Christianity. In the following five centuries, the West exported to the new periphery its model of feudalism, its civilization, and its culture, Romanesque and Gothic art, Renaissance and Reformation.

The rupture came around the year 1500. The demarcation line suddenly reverted to the old Carolingian divide of A.D. 800. Central Europe chose a modified eastern-type answer to the crisis of feudalism described in the western model, a turning point that arrived at its periphery with a delay of two centuries. In the West, the answer was the loosening of the feudal obligations of the peasants, the development of the urban economy, and emergence of precapitalistic elements within a disintegrating feudalism. The eastern periphery, however, chose the opposite way to overcome the crisis with an eastern-type strengthened and brutalized feudalistic structure—the Second Serfdom. With it, East-Central Europe broke away from the West and formed a distinct new region. The break blocked its development for centuries and determined its social, economic, political, and cultural foundations up to the near present as a mixture of eastern and western structures.

The underlying reason for this turnaround was the peripheral situation of the region within the western model. Social structures, which developed organically in the West during half a millennium, from the sixth to the tenth century, were adopted in East-Central Europe in a scant 150 years. Western structural forms evolving in successive phases were transplanted to the periphery in a parallel manner remained incomplete, hybrid and raw, and retained some of its archaic, tribal traits. While, in the West, the main fundamental structures developed spontaneously and the inner organizational principles of the society dominated the state, in East-Central Europe, changes came from above, instead of growing from below.

In contrast to the evolving strength of the autonomous cities in the West, urbanization, and with it an urban market economy, remained rudimentary. In the Hungarian Kingdom, for instance, only a few dozen towns developed, their social role remained insignificant, and no representatives of the towns were ever invited to participate in the Diet, a feudal form of "parliamentary" legislative assembly. The burghers enjoyed rather a higher level of peasant "freedoms" than a lower level of civil freedoms. On the other end of the social scale, due to the rapid inorganic transformation of the initially free middle strata into feudal landlords, the nobility became numerically much stronger than its western counterpart. However, the majority of it retained its essentially peasant character and was unsuitable to fulfill the functions of nobility, though fiercely guarding its privileges and sharply separating itself from the peasantry. While in the West, the nobility constituted about 1 percent of the population, in the East-Central region, its proportion became inflated to 4 or 5 percent in Hungary, even to 7 to 8 percent in Poland. This boorish lower nobility ("gentry" in Hungary, "szlachta" in Poland), full of pretensions and self-importance, became in modern times one of the most harmful obstacles to social development.

In addition to the internal weakness as a periphery to the West, an external influence contributed to the adoption of the Second Serfdom and thus transformed East-Central Europe into a new distinct region, neither West nor East, a mixture in which sometimes one, sometimes the other, dominated during its history. A decisive factor in overcoming the medieval crisis of feudalism in the West was rapid urbanization. With it came a growing demand for agrarian products, a market for which was found in its eastern periphery. To satisfy this demand, the solution of the new region was conforming to its new structural element, the Second Serfdom. Production was increased by developing the demesne agriculture, large noble estates based on forced labor, and the strengthening of feudal oppression of the peasants.

The first signs of the Second Serfdom began simultaneously in East-Central Europe, nearly at the same time. In 1494, by order of the Margrave of Brandenburg in eastern Germany, the peasants were bound to the domain of their landlord, thus giving birth to the Junker class. In Poland, the law of 1496 forbade peasants to leave for town, and a few years later, obligatory labor duty was introduced for up to six days a week. The example was followed in 1497 by Bohemia, at that time ruled by King Wladislaw of Poland. Simultaneously, Wladislaw became also king of Hungary;

he restricted severely the mobility of the peasants, tied them to their landlords, brought back the escaped serfs, introduced forced labor, and deprived them of their right to own land. The law of 1514 codified the "perpetual and universal servitude" of the peasants and, at the same time, declared the nobility the sole legal representative of the country and its "freedom."

The imposition of the Second Serfdom was the decisive moment in the formation of a distinct East-Central European region. It contributed to the slow emergence of the Habsburg Empire and of Prussia and became the underlying factor in the erosion of the economic and social foundation of the independence of Hungary, Bohemia, and Poland.

Between West and East, the region crossed the threshold to the Modern Age under East European conditions, mixed with incomplete, weak western structures. Mainly because of this dichotomy, no uniform model came into being, but distinct variants of it, which retained their separation from West, as well as from East.

The two extreme variants, the Polish Kingdom and the Electorate of Brandenburg, developed in the northern part of the region, an area predestined by its geographical situation at the Baltic Sea. It could adapt itself at the earliest and the fullest to the agricultural and urban-industrial division of labor in the expanding world economy. The seaways from the harbor of Stettin, Gdansk, and Konigsberg offered a preferential transport of grain to the West and compelled this subregion to develop the system in its most consistent, complete form.

In the sixteenth century, the Polish-Lithuanian Kingdom became Europe's largest state, stretching from the Baltic to the Black Sea, from Silesia to the eastern borders of the newly annexed White Russian and Ukrainian plains. Based on the Baltic prosperity and its overwhelming influence in the region, Polish nobility started in an extremist way: on one side, it imposed an increasingly oppressive forced labor on the peasantry, depriving from it the last vestiges of western feudal "freedoms," even in the most private family spheres, and on the other side, it extended its own ambiguous western privileges to the utmost and developed a nobiliary order unknown in the West and the East. The Polish-Lithuanian union rejected any dynastic principle; the king was chosen by and subordinated to the Sejm, the feudal "parliament," dominated exclusively by the nobility.

The Polish submodel formed a reverse structure to the evolving western absolutism and eastern Tsarist autocracy, an attempt to establish a nobiliary absolutism. This takeover of the state power led to a dead end. The general European economic depression at the end of the seventeenth century found in Poland a degenerated urban base, the steep decline of a once blooming feudal culture that had produced a Copernicus in the sciences, a Potecki and Szymonowicz in literature, the fame of Krakow University and its radiance of Renaissance art. The crisis also disrupted the demesne agriculture of the aristocratic estates; the extremist nobiliary "freedom" completely crippled the power of the rulers and paralyzed the functioning of the state. The nobiliary state excluded itself from the "military revolution" of this century, which transformed warfare in the West and in the East. For lack of a trained artillery, even of a standing army, the antiquated cavalry of the landlords were no match for the Swedish, Prussian, Austrian, and Russian armies. The results were the three divisions of Poland from 1772 to 1795 and the disappearance of the country from the map. This East-Central European experience to salvage the western feudal structures, while absurdly overstretching the role of the nobility under eastern structures, ended in failure and catastrophe.

The small Electorate of Brandenburg which, under the House of the Hohenzollern and its ruling Junker class, was the cradle of Prussia, reached a diametrically different conclusion from the eastward turn in the region. At the end of the sixteenth century, the Junkers began to transform their land into large manorial farms by forcibly expropriating the small peasant plots. This starting point of a change to the Second Serfdom was carried out with proverbial German proficiency. Brandenburg completely abandoned the western inheritance and developed the model of an absolutism with a military-bureaucratic structure that had the closest resemblance to the Russian model of all the European absolutisms. By the seventeenth century, the western feudal corporative mechanisms were systematically cut back, the nobility was integrated into the army and administration, and the Junkers became the western counterpart of the Tsarist service nobility.

This structure helped the tiny Brandenburg to a rapid expansion in the western and eastern direction. It organized a formidable standing army, the strongest in medieval Europe, with the Junkers as officers and the serfs as foot soldiers. Frederic William II, the Great, transformed Brandenburg at the turn of the century into the Prussian Kingdom, created a powerful navy, even founded a colony at the African Gold Coast. The feudal landlords had to serve the ruler with unquestioning fealty. Under King Frederic the Great, Prussia occupied Silesia and extended its eastern borders to Warsaw with the annexation of Polish territory.

In his economic policy, he followed an extremist mercantilist course, quite contrary to Poland's antimercantilism. He became the leading representative of the enlightened absolutism in Europe, abolished torture, granted asylum to the French Protestant Huguenot refugees, and gained with them important allies for the spread of capitalistic values. He gathered around his court well-known French scholars, writers, and philosophers, and proclaimed freedom of conscience and religion. Under his rule, Prussia became a great European power, soon to become the main champion of a united Germany.

At the beginning of the eighteenth century, under the curiously contradictory double influence of Napoleon and Tsarist Russia, Prussia chose its specific way of "revolution from above." Though retaining its strict absolutism, in 1807, more than half a century before its Tsarist model, it issued an edict to abolish serfdom, eliminate all feudal, corporative restrictions, and introduced the concept of autonomy of the cities.

The radical Prussian "revolution from above" predestined this model variant of East-Central Europe to bring about the unity of Germany, which—up to 1871—was divided into several hundred territories. It opened the way for a spectacular success of economic catch-up with the West, thus leaving the East-Central region. Success, however, brought its own problems: it eliminated earlier backwardness and other harmful effects of a delayed start in relation to the West, but it also widened the gap between a rapidly modernized economic system and a rather rigid sociopolitical structure inherent in the East-Central region. The traditional ruling class of the Junkers, the landowning and military-bureaucratic elite, had outlived its time, but retained political power and decisive social influence. The success had to remain ambivalent. The ambiguity rests on the deformation in Germany's early history; she had to pay for the fact that her unity came about from "above" and was rooted in the structures of an eastern-type model. The inner obstacles, the weakness of the Weimar democracy, reach back to early modern times. Without this regional inheritance, neither the rise and triumph of fascism, nor the postwar partition, nor the present problems of the new unification of the historically western Federal and the equally historically east-central German Democratic Republic can properly be understood.

Between the two extremes of Poland and Prussia, lies the central region of the dynastic Habsburg Empire which, step-by-step, included Austria proper, the Czech and Hungarian Kingdoms and Polish Galicia. Its structural history is rather contradictory. Until the introduction of the Second Serfdom, in the whole subregion western type feudal structures were preponderant, though from west to east with diminishing strength and increasing delays.

Bohemia and Moravia, since the tenth century a part of the German Kingdom, became at the turn of the fifteenth century engulfed in the Hussite movement, a mixture of religious, Czech nationalstic, and social revolt against the Catholic-German domination. In 1420, it escalated into the Hussite Wars, an essentially peasant uprising under the Protestant flag for the abolition of serfdom, until then the most radical revolt for the destruction of the feudal system in the western region. Only after thirty years of bitter fighting could a Catholic Holy Crusade crush the peasant armies.

The outcome was a politically turbulent period: German, Habsburg, Czech, and Polish rulers succeeded each other, but a religious compromise left Bohemia with a Protestant majority. Another thirty years after the peasant defeat, a radical social turn replaced the antifeudal revolt with a brutal strengthening of feudalism. Under the Polish king Wladislaw a decree was codified in 1487 that introduced the Polish model of Second Serfdom. Royal prerogatives were restricted, the western-type rights of the townsmen curtailed, and the nobility was given hitherto unprecedented power in Bohemia. The sixteenth century added a new momentum to an eastward movement. Now, again under Habsburg rule, conflicts between the Protestant majority and the forcible Counter Reformation of the Austrian Emperors were steadily growing. Within the strengthened East-Central European regional structures, the magnates could extend their large estates only at the expense of the lesser nobility, and labor shortages induced them to further restrict the peasants' freedom of movement. All these religious and social tensions erupted in a new uprising led by the Protestant feudal landlords. Their army of wretched peasants reduced to serfdom was defeated by the Habsburgs in the battle of the White Mountains in 1620.

Revenge was carried out with typical eastern brutality. The leaders of the revolt were executed, the rebels' properties were confiscated, three-quarters of the estates, including those of the Church, changed hands. All nobles refusing Roman Catholicism were expelled from the country; thirty thousand families—a quarter of the nobility and of the urban population—emigrated. This gigantic expropriation and "religious cleansing" created a new administrative-military nobility composed of foreigners, mainly Germans, Spaniards, and Walloons.

In 1627, Emperor Ferdinand II enacted a new constitution. Absolute imperial heredity was established, and Catholicism was proclaimed the sole permitted religion. Legally, the Bohemian lands preserved their independent identity for a short while, but actually they were absorbed into the Habsburg monarchy.

The agrarian structures changed radically. The large feudal estates, which formerly covered one-third of the country, now occupied two-thirds, while the properties of the lesser nobility shrank to insignificance and the cities decayed. With the law of 1680, Second Serfdom was solidly established, forced labor service of the peasants was introduced, beginning with three days a week and rising to six a century later, and their dues multiplied fivefold during this period. The remains of their peasant "freedoms" were erased. The living standard of the serfs fell below the subsistence level, and they even degenerated physically. Bohemia became firmly integrated into the East-Central European region, separated from its western roots.

In the Hungarian Kingdom, the eastward turn was much more sudden. In the fourteenth and fifteenth centuries, the structural tendencies still resembled closely the western model. The development of agrarian techniques and cultivation methods led to a rise in productivity. Serfs began to produce not only for their own personal needs and to bring the ground rent to the landlords, but also for town markets. As part of feudal obligations, money rent more and more replaced the compulsory produce delivery.

While some of the feudal serfs became commodity producers, rid themselves of the most oppressive personal dependencies, and started on the way toward an agrarian-bourgeois development, conflicts and antagonisms sharpened between peasants and landlords. The nobility, keenly aware of those unfolding tendencies, stepped up their feudal exploitation, and compulsory rent increased manifold. The crushing new burdens led to a dramatic impoverishment of the majority of the peasantry. It was this growing oppression that sparked the great peasant uprising of 1514. The peasant army was wiped out by the well-equipped, experienced cavalry of the landlords, and ruthless retaliation followed. The rebel leader, György Dózsa, was burnt alive, and the peasants were murdered and hanged by the thousands.

The vengeance reversed radically western trends and established the Second Serfdom, the typical East-Central European structure, for centuries to come. A long line of decrees imposed new burdens on the serfs and obligated them to render unpaid labor on the estates of the landlords. The nobility was no longer content with limiting their freedom of movement, but abolished it entirely and bound the serfs to the feudal estate. A new law deprived serfs the right to own land and even revoked their hereditary title to their plots. The Act of 1608 took away from the king and the royal administration any judicial power over the peasantry prohibiting any intervention by the central power: the serfs were now exclusively at the mercy of the landlords. From then on, refusal of labor services and escapes were not merely punished by extorting compensation, but were considered sedition, to be dealt with accordingly, even involving the death sentence. The social status of the peasantry came to be defined as "serfs in perpetuity."

The towns lost most of their incipient western-type autonomy. Any nobleman moving into town was exempt from paying taxes, and he was out of reach of urban jurisdiction and regulations. Townspeople lost their monopolistic position in their own markets as landlords dictated prices and took over control of the councils.

The main income of the towns came from the surrounding villages, which now rendered them unpaid labor services. Only those towns that owned villages with serfs could keep some of the previous urban freedoms, that is, they acted as collective landlords.

Notwithstanding all these eastern structural changes, the character of the restored and brutalized medieval serfdom was slightly different from other countries in the region. Grain in Hungary was, at that time, a negligible item in foreign trade, in contrast to Poland and Bohemia. On the other hand, cattle and wine were exported in considerable quantities, and labor services could never be exploited in such a brutal manner in cattle-raising and viniculture as they were in wheat production. The peasants' own production in Hungary suffered severe setbacks, but it did not dwindle to the same extent as in wheat exporting countries.

It was mainly these circumstances that contributed to the fact that in Hungary the feudal ruling class did not succeed in making the system of "perpetual serfdom" completely universal. The resistance of the peasants led to freer development than in other countries of the region, movements into towns could not be halted altogether, and many serfs obtained noble status in return for military services. With the rural burghers of the towns, they constituted a comparatively free peasant strata exempt from the burdens of the Second Serfdom.

Generally, however, by the end of the seventeenth century, Second Serfdom in Hungary triumphed in its most brutal form. Serfs became property of the landlord. They could be exchanged, mortgaged, made a present of, bought and sold, with or without their plot, even without their family.

The picture is seemingly contradictory, but the contradictions merely show the variants of the same complex economic-social category of the Second Serfdom. Hungary followed neither the Prussian variant, an absolutistic royal power with a subservient nobility, nor the Polish one of nobiliary absolutism with a subservient royal power. The Hungarian structure, however, propelled the country toward the same catastrophe as in Poland. The king's power was undermined, most of his revenues taken over by the nobility, so that the royal army, left without pay, began to plunder and was destroyed by the landlord army.

Without the once formidable mercenary royal army, without the massive force of peasants who were crushed following their revolt, the badly trained army of the nobility could not withstand the Turkish onslaught. It was annihilated in the battle of Mohács in 1526. The consequence was the loss of Hungary's independence. The country was divided into three parts: the central, under Turkish occupation; Transylvania in the east, under Turkish protectorate; while the western part, nominally still the "Kingdom of Hungary," became integrated in the Habsburg Empire.

* * *

We shall now proceed to the overall frame of the East-Central European region, the Habsburg Empire, which by the eighteenth century, politically integrated almost the entire region—Austria with its hereditary provinces, Hungary, Bohemia, and Moravia, and the southeastern part of Poland. Only Prussia remained outside and followed its own special path.

This integrative frame is characterized by a peculiarly intermediate, even ambiguous condition concerning the new political map of Europe, between the western and the eastern prototypes. Even the dividing line of Second Serfdom—the river Elbe and the eastern foothills of the Alps—ran through the body of this new blueprint. The agrarian structures of the western hereditary provinces stayed basically closely related to the West. The state structure had, on the one hand, the eastern character of its imperial nature, and on the other hand, it differed sharply from the Russian model, as the imperial centralization remained mostly just an intention up to the end. The dynastic unity, the military and fiscal centralization, was always undermined by the traditional separatism of the individual nations and even provinces, a situation unprecedented in the East, as well as in the West.

Absolutism evolved at the same time and at the same pace as in the western region, but even the first absolutistic turn was accompanied by an eastern type of brutality in Bohemia (1620), and soon after in Hungary (1670), with the bloody repression of an anti-Habsburg conspiracy of the feudal aristocracy.

Hungary is also a good example of the specific central European character of the Habsburg absolutism. Hardly fifty years after the collapse of the aristocratic conspiracy, the feudal nobility launched a war of independence. This time, it ended neither with defeat nor with repression, but with a treaty. The feudal aristocracy accepted a compromise with the Habsburgs. In exchange for recognizing the hereditary succession of the dynasty, the nobility could remain in possession of their estates, enjoy exemptions from taxes, dispose freely of their serfs, and share in government through control of the Hungarian Diet and of the counties that became largely its independent fiefdoms. Such a compromise would have been unimaginable in the East, and again, has no parallel in the West.

The case of Poland is similar. Only fifty years after the final partition of the country, the Polish aristocracy became an important factor in the Vienna parliament. Austrian Galicia got a provincial legislative assembly and a governor appointed from the ranks of Polish aristocrats. With purely Polish administration, schools and courts of law, Galicia became an almost independent Polish state within the empire; its feudal landlords practically governed the country with unlimited control over their serfs.

The political situation concerning the hereditary provinces was also without parallel, either in the West or in the East. They could keep important western feudal structures, the Middle Age–type freedoms of the nobility, of the autonomous cities and of the peasants, while at the same time remaining firmly integrated in dynastic absolutism. In Tyrol and Vorarlberg, peasants even took part in the political administration of the province.

Positioned in the heart of the East-Central European region, the "half-western" structures did not hinder the Habsburg Empire in the eighteenth century from taking up the cause of Enlightenment in a typically "eastern" manner, by imperial order from above, not by a cultural process evolving from below. It became a present of the emperor to "his" peoples, given and taken away at imperial will. Following the introduction of a half-successful, half-failed Enlightenment, the dynasty again made an unequivocal turn to the eastern model when, after the French Revolution, it transformed the absolutistic empire into a "prison of its peoples," similar to Russia.

The ambiguous in-between structure of Austria is also demonstrated clearly in its economic policy. After being politically shut out from western Europe at the conclusion of the Thirty Years' War (1648), the Habsburgs introduced within the narrower frame of their empire the western model of division of labor between center and periphery. The western hereditary provinces became the industrial base, especially Bohemia, where the protoindustrial beginnings in the thirteenth and fourteenth centuries survived within the Second Serfdom and allowed the Habsburgs to develop them consciously into a center of a western-type core. On the other hand, Hungary and Galicia were cast in the role of agrarian colonies.

* * *

We now stop outlining further general social trends and focus on the year 1848, the turning point in the region's history. The revolutions in mid–nineteenth century are as significant for the future development of East-Central Europe as were the "revolutions from above" of the fifteenth century that had given birth to the region. The new revolutions were an exceedingly belated attempt to turn back the clock of history, to reverse Second Serfdom and rejoin the West from which the region had broken off 250 years earlier. Although belated, the time chosen was not arbitrary. The old fetters were ready to burst, the conditions for change were caused by the famous "Springtime of Peoples" with France in its center. The revolutionary zone cut across Europe from Prussia, in the north, to Sicily, in the south. It was the February revolution in France, destroying the Orleanist monarchy and proclaiming the republic, that also triggered the revolutionary explosions in East-Central Europe, mainly in its core, the Habsburg Empire.

In contrast to France, which gave the inspiration, the revolutions of the regions were not bourgeois revolutions in the proper sense, because the region did not have a developed, powerful bourgeoisie. Nor were they capitalist-industrial revolutions of the English model, because the feudal ruling classes had no capital accumulated to invest in a modernization of their outdated, underdeveloped economy. The intermediate structures of the region between East and West—the multinational composition of the Habsburg Monarchy—lent the revolutions a specific national, social, and political content that swept away the feudal system and made possible the future capitalist transformation, but with a semibourgeois, semifeudal distorted character. Vienna and Prague came closest to the French model, with an ascending bourgeoisie and an incipient working class whose participation in the revolution foreshadowed the development of Austria, and especially Czechoslovakia, after World War I into a capitalistic system more or less free of serious distortions. It enabled them to develop democracy that was missing in all the other countries of the region.

To get the region out of its backwardness, the feudal system had to be broken; modernization required the abolition of serfdom within a progressive, liberal political framework. This requirement had been fulfilled only partially—in all the revolutions of the region political change had been ultimately suppressed by the old order.

The 1848 revolutions in the region were all "revolutions from above," starting and ending at the top. It was the farsighted wing of the aristocracy that demanded changes to reform and modernize the stagnating feudal system, but without endangering their own rule. However, this aristocracy did not succeed in keeping the process it started under control, and the changes were taken over by the declining gentry and the upcoming urban classes. Finally, royal power and aristocracy brutally suppressed the revolutions and reverted them to the original intention, a modernized postfeudal version of the old.

In Vienna, the prelude to the revolution was a plot of reform-minded aristocrats to oust Prince Metternich, the main representative of social and political backwardness. In the wake of the inspiring news of the February revolution in France, their reform promises were the spark that ignited the restless, hungry urban proto-"proletariat," landless laborers who were looking for work in Vienna, but could find no capitalists to employ them. The unorganized riots found their leaders in the university students who demanded a liberal constitution with universal suffrage, abolition of *robot*, feudal forced labor. On March 13, 1848, barricades went up in the streets. During the next few months, revolutionary fever engulfed Vienna; on May 17, the imperial court fled from the capital. Two days later, the power passed to a Committee of Public Safety, headed by students and moderate liberals. In July, the frightened parliament saved imperial rule by choosing a somewhat more liberal cabinet and accepting a few peasants and burghers among its members. The reformed parliament offered and got granted a double compromise to turn the people's revolution into a "revolution from above." The liberals accepted the empire and the dynasty; the dynasty accepted liberalism. In September, it issued the Act of Emancipation that abolished the hereditary rights of landlords in jurisdiction and administration; it abolished *robot* and gave the peasant tenants security, even on the lord's land. With this, the threat of a peasant uprising had been averted. The threat of a victorious bourgeois revolution remained, but after only one month this, too, was resolved when the imperial army destroyed the revolutionary forces in Vienna, internally disunited by conflicts between the radicals and the moderates.

The immediate victor was the imperial regime, which did not keep its liberal political promises and resumed an absolutistic course. The landlord class lost inefficient feudal service, but this was vastly outweighed by the gains in modernization of their estates. With compensation money received for losing their serfs, they could now engage in commerce and industry and buy up additional peasant and gentry property. The peasants' victory was also ambiguous. They were freed from feudal obligations by the grace of the emperor and his aristocrat allies; however, many lost their newly won properties to big landowners. Small peasant holdings could not compete with the agrotechnical progress of the large estates, and they became pauperized. Neither cotters nor agricultural laborers were allotted any land by the emancipation act. The long-term victor was capitalism. In the following decades, industrial production showed a rapid increase. The banking system grew by leaps and bounds, and it became the principal source of industrialization, railway buildings, and agricultural modernization.

The Hungarian revolution was deeper, wider, and longer than the Austrian one. While the Austrian revolution remained largely restricted to Vienna, revolution in Hungary engulfed the whole country. In Vienna, social and political change fueled the revolution; in Hungary the additional demand for liberation from Austrian domination expanded it into a war of independence.

The prelude was similar to that in Vienna. The initiative for economic and institutional reform came from Count István Széchenyi, a member of one of the most prestigious aristocratic families. He called for the modernization of backward Hungary by granting all inhabitants equality before the law and including the prosperous farmers and the rising class of entrepreneurs in the political nation. All these reforms had to be achieved within the "continued preponderance of the landowning classes, the sole guarantors for the survival of the nation" (Janos 1982, 57). He rejected the idea of a constitutional monarchy and called it "a torch in the hands of arsonists" (Janos 1982, 53), and never demanded full autonomy or independence for Hungary.

It was the lower nobility, the gentry, that complemented social reform with the protest against Habsburg oppression, a change of balance between Austria and Hungary, also between church and state, aristocrat and common nobleman. The nation should become a Magyar ethnic community. Political rights should be extended to classes outside of the feudal privileged ones. The gentry was a class in decline, on the verge of economic ruin; it consisted of marginal landowners plagued by constant pecuniary problems. It abhorred "demeaning" entrepreneurship, its liberal demands aimed at a strong state that provided security of employment in the bureaucracy and in politics. It asked not only economic reforms, but also national independence, power, and prestige.

The backbone of the radical faction consisted of the rising noble and urban intelligentsia, students, such petty nobles as Lajos Kossuth (a lawyer and journalist), and the impoverished Baron József Eötvös, or the gentry Mór Jókai, both making ends meet as novelists. A nonnoble exception and the most radical among them was the poet Sándor Petőfi, son of a provincial butcher. The bourgeoisie played hardly any role in the reform movement. The old commercial and protoindustrial urban stratum, mostly of German origin, was in steep decline, and lost even the little influence they had in the city of Pest. The new upcoming bourgeoisie was preponderantly Jewish and prudently avoided mixing into politics.

Two days after the news of the revolution in Vienna reached Hungary, on March 15, 1848, demonstrations took place in Buda and Pest. A mass of rioters, led by the poet Petofi, demanded freedom and political rights for the people, proclaimed the revolution, and organized a Revolutionary Committee. The Diet, the Hungarian parliament, fearing that the urban uprising would spread to the countryside and lead to a serf insurrection, convened immediately and under the leadership of Kossuth, formed a new government that issued six legislative acts that completely changed the political and social structure of the country. They abolished serfdom and the tax exemption of the nobility, replaced the noble Diet by a bicameral National Assembly, the House of Lords, and a House of Representatives with elected members. The law guaranteed the right to vote to all male citizens over twenty years of age but made some important exceptions. It connected this right with several economic qualifications, mainly ownership of land and other property and thus enfranchised 6.5 percent of the population. The law redefined the relationship of the country within the Habsburg Empire by increasing the autonomy of Hungary and establishing separate Hungarian ministries of defense and finance.

These last provisions were immediately rejected by the emperor. He fomented an armed rebellion among the Croatian and Rumanian inhabitants of Hungary, dismissed the revolutionary government, and ordered the dissolution of the National Assembly. The parliament answered with the dethronement of the emperor and began to organize a national army which, in the ensuing war of independence, destroyed the military assault of the Croats and allowed Hungarian troops recruited among the enthusiastic peasant masses to repulse the invading Austrian army. The revolution was defeated only when Vienna called in Russian forces. On August 31, 1849, the revolutionary army capitulated—not to the Austrians, but to the Russian commander.

Alone among the revolutions in 1848, the Hungarian one did not fall by internal weakness and conflicts, but by overpowering military conquest. It was also the longest one in the region, lasting for seventeen months. Its exceptional strength was due to the combination of national and social liberation, since the peasants received their freedom, not from the king, but from the Hungarian nation.

After the defeat of the revolution, Hungary lost its independence and was incorporated into the now even more repressive Habsburg Monarchy. Though the emancipation law had been retained, only the land formerly worked by feudal statute forced labor passed into peasant ownership. The former landlords kept their estates; more than half of the total land remained in their hands while more than half of the peasantry owned no land at all. Capitalist development started much later and slower than in Austria, mainly with the aid of Austrian capital. Hungary remained backward, underdeveloped, semicolonial, and semifeudal until the upheavals following World War I significantly changed the structures of the independent, vastly shrunken country.

The Austrian and Hungarian revolutions were the most important ones in East-Central Europe. But there were revolts and revolutions in the entire region. Prague was stirred by the "Springtime of Peoples" a few days before the revolutionary outbreak in Vienna and Budapest. Nationalistic demonstrations led by students demanded the equal use of the Czech and German language in schools and public offices. In the following months, the mood became more and more aggressive, with demands including general voting rights, greater autonomy for Bohemia, and the abolition of the feudal forced labor. Students were joined by workers and lower intellectuals, and the initially passive peasants became restless. To isolate the radicals from their rural base, in a successfully tested "revolution from above," the Viennese imperial government freed the peasants from feudal obligations. But urban nationalism with bourgeois overtones seemed to it more dangerous, and thus it sent troops to Prague. It was this provocative move that transformed the ongoing peaceful demonstrations and petitions into an open riot. On June 12, 1848, Czech students and workers set up barricades, and fights broke out. Austrian troops occupied the university, and in pitched battles lasting four days, they bloodily suppressed the short "Whitsuntide Revolution"—but not without the support of the loyal German middle class.

In the Habsburg province of Polish Galicia, a peculiar alliance developed in the 1840s between the serfs and the occupying Austrians against the nationalist-revolutionary movement of the Polish nobility. The Habsburg camarilla undertook the easy task of instigating a serf uprising, the only pure peasant revolt in the region, which was bloodily crushed in 1846 by the Polish aristocrats. The imperial government thanked the peasants for their loyal cooperation and ordered the abolition of the feudal *robot*. With it, the Habsburgs detached the peasants from the nobility and made assurances that no revolution could take place in Poland, only an isolated uprising in Krakow that was suppressed in two days by the military.

The farthest the revolutionary wave reached in the region was the short-lived insurrection in the Danubian principalities Moldavia and Walachia, the cradle of Rumania. The uprising of the lesser nobility against the ruling boyars was quickly and brutally suppressed by the joint Russian and Turkish armies.

The twin principalities were the only country in the region where, after the defeat of the revolution, feudalism was not dismantled, but on the contrary, became more oppressive with the late introduction of a Russian-type Second Serfdom. By August 1849, with the capitulation of the Hungarian army, all the revolutionary flames were extinguished by military force. The power of the absolutist Habsburg Empire was restored, even strengthened, with the aristocracy regaining its domination. Virtually all the institutional changes, all the political and social dreams, were wiped out. There was, however, one exception—the only major irreversible change: the abolition of serfdom in the Habsburg Monarchy. The door was now open for the social transformation of the East-Central European region. In the following decades, this crucial change fulfilled, though only partially and with a distorted character, some of the promises that the revolutions of 1848 could not achieve.

* * *

With the abolition of serfdom, a rapid capitalist transformation set in within Austria proper. The main impulse came from banking that had made Vienna, in the first half of the nineteenth century, the financial center of the empire and had played an important role in the whole of Europe. The Viennese branch of the Rothschild House rose to a special eminence and after midcentury, changed the traditional feudal credit operations into the German- and French-type of capitalist loans as the principal source of financing the economy. Soon Austria became not only receiver, but also an exporter of capital.

Industrial production increased two and a half times between 1840 and 1880, and another four times until 1913. The structure of the economy and the distribution of the working population became comparable to that of France. Austria was on its way to leaving the East-Central region and joining the West. The rupture would have come, had Austria not had to carry with her the preponderantly agrarian Hungary, Galicia, and Bukovina, where feudal structures clung stubbornly to the social body, even after the emancipation of the serfs.

The defeat in World War I and the dismemberment of the Habsburg Empire thrust Austria into a disastrous position. The Viennese population suffered from hunger; bread, flour, and milk were hardly enough to prevent its people from starvation. The country was practically cut off from the other parts of the former monarchy, which had gotten its coal from Silesia and its grain from Hungary. In the textile industry, spinning had been done in western Austria, weaving in Bohemia, and the clothing manufacturers were in Vienna. However, with the massive financial help of the West, capitalist development soon resumed and proceeded at a fast pace. Right before the *Anschluss* to Hitler's Germany, industrial production per capita equaled that of Hungary, Poland, Rumania, and Bulgaria combined, though it reached only half of the level in the developed region of Europe. Economically, Austria became part, even if a peripheral one, of the West.

Politically and socially, however, its east-central Habsburgian roots remained very much manifest in the widespread absence of national consciousness, weak democracy, and persistent anti-Semitism, to state the most obvious characteristic features. A strong rightist movement, with no parallel in western democracies, led to outright "Austro-Fascism" that destroyed with armed force the socialist resistance. It was partly this East-Central heritage that explains the easy submission of the country to German Nazi expansionism.

Only after Hitler's defeat did this heritage fade, though not completely. The specific Habsburgian compromise character reappears in the *Sozialpartnerschaft* between state, industry, and trade union, as well as in the corporatist structures of the economy. However, since World War I, Austria has been unequivocally part of the western region. That is why the country ceases to be a subject of this book.

Let us now turn back to Hungary. The abolition of serfdom in the revolution of 1848 bore the stamp of its "eastern" character; the domination by the wealthy nobility was unbroken. Close to two-thirds of the land remained in the hands of former feudal landlords, mostly the 160 families that made up the great aristocratic clans of the kingdom. At the same time, the formal freeing of the serfs left 60 percent of them landless. On the other side, in the following decades, the great magnates succeeded in increasing their estates enormously. The area covered by farms above 15,000 acres grew in the period 1867–1914 from 8.5 percent of the area of the landed property to 19.4 percent.

Hungary remained a preponderantly agricultural appendix of the Habsburg Empire. Its ambiguous structural variant of the regional model survived the revolution of 1848 and the abolition of serfdom; it salvaged to a significant extent its prerevolutionary structures, and it preserved the weakened, but not severed, colonial bonds to Vienna. As we will show, capitalist tendencies in agriculture tried to gain strength in the last quarter of the century, but only in a deformed manner, interwoven with feudal elements. Modern industry began to develop, from practically zero before 1848, to 20 percent of the national product at the turn of the century, but still far behind even Austria proper. No national bourgeoisie developed. Industry, finance, and trade remained professions "beyond the dignity" of the low and high nobility alike, and peasants were excluded from them, their place taken by Germans and mainly Jews. Hungary entered the twentieth century with the dead weight of the past obstructing and distorting all progress.

A different pattern characterized the structural development of Bohemia. As we have seen, the initial model of western-type feudalism evolved much earlier and faster than in other countries of the future central region. Alongside the independent peasant holding, paying rent in cash and in kind as the dominant element, landlords were involved as early as the Middle Ages in precapitalist manufacturing and in the trade of food and textile products. The emergence of this precapitalist nobility prepared the way for the conversion of a significant number of landlords and the majority of the population, to Protestantism.

The defeat of the Czech nobility by the Habsburgs in the Battle of White Mountain, in 1620, put an end to Bohemia's independence, and the introduction of the Second Serfdom cut short the development toward a western-type feudal structure. History, however, assigned a special place to this new imperial acquisition. The Habsburgs soon recognized the inherent possibilities for the region and cast the Bohemian province in the role of their main industrial core.

The Czech nobility traditionally did not share the disdain for work of its Hungarian counterpart, and they became, by the eighteenth century, the major entrepreneurs in the growing protoindustries. In the same century, Maria Theresa limited the unpaid labor services of the serfs, then Joseph II created a more mobile labor force with his partial "emancipation." Forced labor obligations were not abolished, but serfs were now permitted to marry without seeking permission; they could move if they were not indebted to their landlord, learn trades and arts without payment to, or even consent of, the landlord. In contrast to Hungary, the loosening of Second Serfdom from above was not sabotaged by a dominant "national" aristocracy. Both the Crown and the cosmopolitan imperial nobility encouraged protoindustrialization, the Habsburgs to strengthen their empire, the nobility to increase their income.

At the turn of the nineteenth century, mechanical devices started to change manufacturing, and in the next decades, a rapidly growing cotton and linen industry developed. Nonnoble entrepreneurs began to overtake the aristocracy, and an increasing number of merchants, rich peasants, and prosperous artisans created a fastgrowing middle layer with many characteristics of a bourgeoisie. By the time of the 1848 revolution and the abolition of all remnants of serfdom, the road was wide open for capitalist development. A unique structural evolution, made possible by the oppression of its national feudal ruling class and by the imperial division of labor, predestined the Czech lands, after the disintegration of the Habsburg Empire, to enter independence in 1918 as a full member of the western region.

The scope and intentions of this book do not allow us to follow the short life of Czechoslovakia during the interwar years. We will pick up the broken thread in 1945, when the resurrected country chose to be a bridge between East and West. In 1948, when the Cold War made the gap unbridgeable, choice was no longer possible, Czechoslovakia was incorporated into the eastern region, together with the Stalinized countries of East-Central Europe.

4

The Balkan Subregion

A PERIPHERY OF EAST-CENTRAL EUROPE

Around the decades of mid–nineteenth century, when Prussia, Bohemia, and Austria started on the road away from structural East-Central Europe, history offered a compensation. The region began to expand southward and pulled the Balkans, southeastern "Europe," into its orbit.

The Balkan Peninsula's place was, until the nineteenth century, only geographically identified in southeastern Europe. Since the formation of Europe after the dissolution of the Roman Empire, the southern border of the West, Center, and East ended here for a thousand years. It was blocked first by the Byzantine Empire with its center in Constantinople, then by the Ottoman Sultanate when, at the end of the Middle Ages, Islamic Turks drove a wedge from the Middle East into the Balkan Peninsula, overthrew Byzantium, and established their empire.

The doors to Europe opened only after a long series of wars, which ranged from the seventeenth to the nineteenth centuries when Austrian and Russian armies drove the Turks back to Asia Minor. The independence of the Balkan kingdoms belongs to modern history: Greece achieved it in 1829, Rumania and Serbia in 1878; in the same year Russia grabbed Dobruja; Bulgaria became independent in 1908; Bosnia was annexed to the Habsburg Empire in 1878; and Macedonia was divided in 1913 between Greece, Serbia, and Bulgaria. The new states became pawns in the antagonistic political, economic, and strategic ambitions of the Great Powers—Austria, Russia, Italy, England, and France. Only after World War I did history place those countries firmly in the periphery of East-Central Europe, as a distinct subregion.

In the sixth century, nomadic Slavic and Turkish tribes poured from the east in to the Balkans. The next century saw the establishment of the Bulgar Khanate, which expanded into a mighty empire, occupying the whole peninsula from the northern borders of today's Greece deep into the Danubian basin. In the ninth century, the empire embraced Eastern Christianity, and the nomadic natural economy began to develop feudal traits. The evolution was halted by incessant wars against the expanding Byzantium which, in 1014, put an end to the independence of Bulgaria. With the occupation of the Serb Kingdom, the empire completed its rule over the Balkans. Only Croatia remained outside and was annexed to Hungary.

When the empire began to disintegrate under Turkish pressure, Bulgaria and Serbia regained their independence for a short time, but the destruction of agriculture during the constant warfare, geographic isolation, and finally depopulation caused by the bubonic plague, made them easy prey to Islamic conquest. One after the other, the Balkan countries fell under Turkish rule—Serbia in 1389, Bulgaria in 1393, and Greece in 1458.

Under the Ottoman Empire, military oppression and the merciless extraction of ransoms and levies weighed heavily on the population. The conquerors transformed the existing socioeconomic system. Traditional forms of class and the mixture of natural and feudal economy disappeared, while the dominant Turkish feudalism preserved many elements of its Asiatic heritage.

The principal feature was maximal centralization, based on the concentration of land ownership in the hands of the state. The landlord-serf relationship assumed thereby a special nature. The Turkish landlords appointed by the sultan exercised only a controlling function, securing an income fixed by the state. Under this system, the peasant masses became a state peasantry, serfs of the ruler. The landlord was a state official without ownership and without the right of holding the estate for life or inheriting land by way of succession.

Due to the Turkish system of feudalism, commercial agriculture did not develop on the large estates, and urban advance was exceedingly slow. The result of the extortive and exploitative government taxation and finance was a stagnation of socioeconomic development for centuries. Turkish feudalism was characterized not only by backwardness, even in comparison to the Eastern and East-Central European regions, but also by excessive rigidity and hardly any capacity for response to external challenges. Hence, the general European advance that began with the fifteenth century created little, if any, stir in the Ottoman Sultanate. The Turkish type of feudalism, a "state command economy," was irreconcilably antagonistic to European feudal structures, were they of protocapitalistic western, autocratic eastern, or mixed central type. It remained intact and shut the Balkans off from other regions until the decline of the Ottoman Empire.

The slow weakening and shrinking of the empire began in the early nineteenth century and ended with the expulsion of the Turks from the Balkans. In its last stage, between 1840 and 1879, laws in Serbia put the land step-by-step into the possession of the peasants. In Bulgaria, the Ottoman feudal system collapsed suddenly after 1879 when, as the result of the Turkish-Russian war, not only Turkish landowners, but also the majority of Turkish peasants fled the country. The Bulgarian peasants were freed from the vestiges of feudal conditions and could easily acquire new plots of land. Even the remaining Turkish landowners were compelled to hand their property over to the peasants. By the end of the century, 88 percent of the farms were small plots under 10 hectares and in peasant ownership, only 0.1 percent of the holdings exceeded 100 hectares.

Serbian land distribution was nearly identical. By their entry into the twentieth century, the agrarian structure of both countries was marked by the full domination of peasant farmers. Agrarian capitalist impulses rested on a base of small holdings.

Walachia and Moldavia, the precursors of Rumania, appeared late on the European scene, in the thirteenth century. East of the

Carpathian Mountains, the rise of organized societies and economies was long delayed by the continued migration of nomadic peoples—Hungarians, Cumans, Jazygs, Petchenegs, and Bulgarians.
The economy of the Rumanian plain was still predominantly pastoral, and the population was living in semipermanent settlements.
In the fourteenth century, when the two principalities were formed,
some progress had begun as cereal production and transit trade
between Novgorod and the Levant developed. On the one hand,
under Bulgarian influence, Byzantine Christianity was adopted; on
the other hand, under Russian influence, a primitive form of eastern feudalism took shape as the communal villages made payments
to the boyar nobility.

A century later, Turkish expansion led to the incorporation of
both principalities into the Ottoman Empire. However, the Turkish
type of feudalism never became as strong as in the provinces south of
the Danube. The boyars sharpened the exploitation of the peasants
systematically, but serfdom remained incomplete, partly because of
the low population density and partly because of the ability of the
peasants to flee to mountainous regions. Also, the fact that most of
the trade was in livestock, including sheep that were raised by trans-
humance, kept the peasants in constant motion and made it difficult
for the boyars to tie them down to one place for long.

The Ottoman rule froze social conditions, so that when, in the
fifteenth and sixteenth centuries, Second Serfdom reached Eastern
and East-Central Europe, here in Wallachia and Moldavia, there
was no need to introduce it. Feudalism remained unbroken. In the
seventeenth century, most of the plains came under boyar control,
although not in the form of ownership. Instead, they controlled the
villages, became their "masters," collected a tithe, and extracted
labor services from the peasants.

With the weakening of the Ottoman occupation in the next century, the structure of the ruling class changed. The Turks employed
Greeks from the Phanar district of Constantinople as their agents.
The Phanariot princes forced the boyars to lease them their lands
and, with this, took over control of the villages from them. The
tenure of the Phanariots was of short duration, but they increased
sharply the exploitation of the serfs and remained powerful landlords and political figures deep into the nineteenth century. Thus
the boyars were downgraded to the second social level and to com-

pensate their economic decline, raised the tithes of the peasants from one-tenth to one-fifth.

The partial opening of the closed Turkish feudal system, with its peculiar vagueness of ownership concept, was accomplished by the growing Russian expansionist pressure on the Ottoman Empire. A short Tsarist occupation of Moldavia and Walachia ended in a joint Turkish-Russian rule and led, in 1830, to the promulgation of the Organic Statutes, a late "Rumanian" version of the Second Serfdom. It abolished the Turkish monopoly of foreign trade and gave the two principalities a rudimentary system of public administration in which the boyars, until then only princely retainers with certain privileges in exchange for services, became a hereditary nobility.

The Organic Statutes sharply increased social antagonism. Previously, average boyar families lived in simple wooden houses without glass windows and wore Turkish-style caftans. Western fashions, "luxuries" such as watches, silverware, lamps, mirrors, and manufactured household items were unknown except to the most prosperous aristocrats. After 1830, the boyars began to build brick houses and to acquire all those "luxuries," which were by that time already common articles of consumption among their western, east-central, eastern upper, and even middle classes. For the boyars, however, these costly articles represented an intolerable financial burden. To enlarge their estates, they intensified the exploitation of the serfs, but even so many were plunged into indebtedness and financial ruin.

The masses of the peasantry did not take part in these developments. Here and there the traditional hovels were replaced by houses with windows and chimneys, but they knew only wheat, bread, sugar, or kerosene from the houses of their masters. The boyars shifted some of their own burdens onto the shoulders of the serf-tenants, raised dues and taxes, enlarged their estates or augmented the unpaid servile labor. Many peasants simply dropped out of the production process, escaped to the forests, and took up a life of banditry.

The economic decline of the lower nobility on the brink of bankruptcy gave rise to a reform movement led by the lesser boyars. Pressure for reform also came from fear of pilfering and murdering by bands of escaped peasants; those *haiduci* were so numerous that many landowners abandoned their estates and settled in the relative safety of Bucharest.

The demands for social reform and national liberation were cut short in 1848 when the uprising, triggered by the revolution in neighboring Hungary and led by the lesser nobility, was suppressed by a joint Russo-Turkish military intervention. The Organic Statutes were restored, and the principalities remained under the suzerainty of the sultan.

The social backwardness of Walachia and Moldavia remained staggering. Agriculture was not only preponderant, but also biblical in its primitiveness. Wooden plows were prevalent, systematic crop rotation was absent, and the great shortage of fertilizers and beasts of burden seemed to place the methods of production on a par with conditions prevailing in the West in the twelfth and thirteenth centuries.

Reforms could be delayed but not avoided amidst a rapidly changing world. The two principalities became unified in 1859 under the name of Rumania, though full independence from Ottoman rule and Tsarist protectorate came only years later, in 1878, after the end of the Russian-Turkish war. Social reforms soon followed. The law of 1864 decreed a partial liberation of the serfs from unpaid forced labor, but left many feudal characteristics intact. The reform spelled out for the first time the concept of ownership, which by the end of the century, allowed for less than 1 percent of the new owners to appropriate nearly half of the total land area, while the mass of the poor peasants were left with tiny plots hardly large enough to feed them. Due to its specific mixture of Central European, Turkish, and Russian semifeudalism, the agrarian economy lagged far behind. The capital stock in agriculture remained one of the lowest in Europe, not only in comparison to the West, but also to Hungary and even to Bulgaria.

As in the Hungarian kingdom, the Rumanian nobility found commerce and industry "unsuitable for a gentleman." The lesser boyars moved into the state bureaucracy and the military; the thin layer of great landowners resided in Bucharest and handed their estates to the care of managers. In the void left by the boyars, mostly Jews, Greeks, Armenians, and Germans filled the role of capitalist entrepreneurs in the agrarian sector as lessors of the estates, and held in their hands the network of merchants and traders to send the grain to the international market.

The Rumanian constitution of 1866, in force until 1923, denied Jews the right to own land. They could not become citizens and were prohibited from settling in the countryside. Restricted to the towns and cities, they became artisans, traders, and bankers, and played a decisive role in the early capitalist development. By the end of the century, Jews made up three-fourths of the work force employed in industry, trade, and credit.

As late as 1913, less than 1 percent of the economically active population was engaged in manufacture and industry, and among them, only a small fraction could qualify as modern industrial workers. Add to this the fact that even the minuscule embryonic industry was almost completely built with foreign—mainly Austrian—capital and owned at an unprecedentedly high ratio of 92 percent by foreigners.

Rumania, Serbia, and Bulgaria entered the twentieth century with an extremely unfavorable historical, social, and economic background. Only decades ago, world politics opened the gates to Europe for them, brought them independence, and blocked their way to be absorbed into the Russian region. They came to be attached to East Central Europe as its most backward eastern periphery. Neither the beginning capitalist, nor the following Soviet-type "socialist" period could overcome this historically determined peripheral position, a legacy of having been excluded from Europe for a thousand years.

* * *

This chapter, about the inclusion of the Balkan countries in the East-Central European region ends without any mention of Greece. Some explanation might be necessary. Its precapitalist history, its socioeconomic structure, did not differ basically from that of other Balkan countries, neither in the Turkish-feudal, nor in the capitalist period. What sets it apart, at least for this book (it will also be omitted in all the following chapters) is its political history.

By the time it regained independence in 1829, Greece occupied a special place. Alone among the Balkan peoples, its struggle against Turkish occupation was fused with the ideas of the French Revolution. It became the myth and inspiration of western European liberals. Their support, a kind of early International Brigade, was of very considerable assistance in winning independence. For Britain, there were not only ideological and sentimental reasons to come to the aid of Greece; Britain had a vital interest in putting up a barrier to Russian ambitions for the Levant by erecting an independent Greek nation. Greece became, and remained, of eminent strategic importance for British control of the Mediterranean. Its geographical position helped it to develop a bourgeoisie much earlier and faster than in other Balkan states, and made it a leader in commerce and shipping. On the other hand, sharpening social tensions led to the development of the strongest Communist Party in the Balkans of the interwar period. In the last years of World War II, Communist-led partisans forced the Germans to retreat from Greece, and in the following civil war, only British and American armed intervention forestalled their seizure of power.

Stalin's decision during the Moscow Conference in October 1944—to give the West a free hand in Greece and leave the Communists to their fate—put Greece in the unique position in the Balkans to keep its special East-Central backward social structure, but at the same time, assigned it politically to the Mediterranean region, together with Italy, Spain, and Portugal. It is this ambivalent situation that induced the author not to include Greece in this book, as was also done by most other historians of East-Central Europe (e.g., F. Rothschild and I. T. Berend).

5

From Dependency to Statism

THE WAY TOWARD CATASTROPHE

In the mid–nineteenth century, the differences of western and East-Central Europe were staggering. The gross national income of the central region reached just 40 percent of the West, but even this low rate blurs the real magnitude of backwardness. The western countries were well advanced in their capitalist development; the industrial share was 23 percent in France, 30 percent in Belgium, and 40 percent in Great Britain. The two seceding countries from the central region, Germany and Austria, rushed to catch up with the West. Just three decades later, the volume of per capita gross national product of a unified Germany already surpassed that of France; Austria, with Bohemia, reached the level of Holland and Sweden.

At the same point, East-Central Europe was still stuck in a rigid feudal and preponderantly agrarian system. Modern industry was practically absent. In partitioned Poland, neither the Prussian nor the Austrian and Russian occupiers tolerated the rise of any industrial competition. In Hungary, it was only in the 1840s that laws allowed nonnobles to establish some factories and, altogether, only nine steam engines were installed using a total of 100 horsepower. In the Rumanian principalities and the other Balkan countries, industry was completely unknown.

The late dawn of capitalism reached the region with 80 to 90 percent of the population living by the land when, at the same time, in the West, the agrarian share was 30 to 40 percent, and in Britain, just 9 percent and rapidly diminishing. In Hungary and Rumania, the legal abolishment of serfdom left the land distribution hardly changed; 53 to 60 percent of the land remained the property of the former feudal landlords, and their huge holdings kept growing. In Hungary and in partitioned Poland, just 16 percent of the arable land was owned by individual peasants, in tiny plots hardly sufficient to feed them. In Rumania it was only 5 percent. In all three big estate countries, 40 to 60 percent of the former serfs entered freedom without any land at all—a socially explosive mass of occasionally hired or permanently unemployed agrarian proletariat.

In the Balkan countries of Bulgaria and Serbia, the Ottoman conquest annihilated the indigenous medieval nobility, and Turkish-type feudalism did not recreate a new class of big estate proprietors. The two countries began their independence with a land distribution of which close to 90 percent of the farms consisted of small plots on mere subsistence level.

The backwardness of agricultural East-Central Europe is well illustrated by the abysmally low rate of literacy. At the turn of the century, only 1 to 2 percent of the adult population were illiterate in Great Britain, Holland, Germany, Switzerland, and the Scandinavian countries, while in Hungary, the relatively "advanced" eastern part of the Habsburg Empire, only one-third could read and write. In the Polish territories, Rumania, Bulgaria, and Serbia, the rate was 20 to 25 percent, at about the same level as the average in today's Africa.

The beginnings of capitalist development in the West reach back to the late Middle Ages. The response to the crises in the fourteenth and fifteenth centuries led, as we have seen, to a slow, gradual loosening of feudalism. Market relations in agriculture and rapid urbanization undermined the system and, centuries later, dissolved it.

The breakthrough came in Britain and was made possible by the original accumulation of capital over the centuries which, in the late 1700s, produced sufficient means for the surge of an all-encompassing industrialization, the backbone of capitalism.

In the continental West, the Industrial Revolution exploded decades later, and precapitalist accumulation remained at a much lower level. It was supplemented by the evolution of a specific domestic banking system (Credit Mobilier in France, Preussische Staatsbank in Germany, the Vienna branch of the Rothschilds in Austria, etc.). This system was designed to collect, concentrate, and finance not just individual entrepreneurs, but the long-term investment needs of the overall economy.

The East-Central European region followed a different path. In the emergence and development of capitalism, it also kept its separateness and distinct differences from the West and the East. The impulse for a capitalist opening came from the developed West. The region had to dismantle feudalism to avert complete social, economic, political, and military insignificance. In the second half of the nineteenth century, the main preconditions to break out of immobility and backwardness were enforced from outside, from above, and from below: socioeconomically, serfdom was abolished; politically, Hungary achieved a considerable measure of autonomy through compromise with Austria; and the Balkan countries regained their independence from Ottoman rule. Only the dismembered Poland had to wait another fifty years for its rebirth. East-Central Europe finally stood at the threshold of the capitalist era.

The threshold, however, could not be crossed unaided. As we have seen, the specific structure of Second Serfdom did not give rise to a domestic bourgeoisie, to an increasingly free peasantry, or to commercially minded feudal landlords. Incipient urbanization had been stopped five hundred years before. There was no self-generated precapitalist accumulation necessary for the transition. It was the influx of foreign capital that substituted for it and gave the impulse to modernization, assisted by the state power of emerging countries of the region.

After World War I, the roles were reversed; gradually state intervention became the main substitute while the productive impact of foreign capital receded. In the prewar period, western capital served the economic transition; in the interwar decades, however, its direction changed and foreign loans were steered mainly to overcome the initial disintegration and to finance the subsequent reconstruction of the war-ravaged countries of East-Central Europe. At the same time, loans served to gain political influence in the radically transformed region.

For closing the gap between the backward region and the West, a strong domestic capitalist class—a well-functioning bourgeoisie and free market economy—would have been necessary. Postwar East-Central Europe had neither. The belated start and feudal hold-overs obstructed sufficient accumulation. The role of the dried-up substitute, productive foreign capital, was taken over by the state that served its increasingly autocratic economy, its militaristic, anti-Semitic, revanchistic political course. Eventually, state interference gave East-Central Europe its specific structural characteristic: a distorted capitalism interwoven with feudal remnants, unstable, undemocratic, the "crisis zone of Europe," as I. T. Berend pertinently called it.

The beginnings were promising. Foreign capital started to flow into the region in the middle of the nineteenth century, triggered by the grain hunger of rapidly industrializing Austria and Bohemia. The main recipient was Hungary, due to its customs union with the western part of the Habsburg Empire. Foreign mortgage loans shot up from 30 million to 3.5 billion crowns in just a few decades, and wheat production and export doubled and tripled. Mechanization of agriculture and the use of chemical fertilizers rose spectacularly, although the upsurge is deceptive, considering the abysmally low starting point. In Rumania and in Hungary, foreign mortgage loans went preponderantly to former feudal landlords with large estates, but only a small fraction was spent for productive investments. Yield increases were achieved mainly by enlarging the arable land and buying up the properties of poor and middle peasants and of the lesser nobility. The bulk of the loan and of the profit from the export boom were spent for an even more luxurious lifestyle.

Much more important for the overall development of the economy was the role of foreign capital in the establishment of a modern transport and credit system, which was connected with the beginning of industry and mining. Here, western capital became the dominant factor. Its influx was closely linked to the agrarian structure, to the natural resources of the region; grain, oil, minerals, and timber had to be forwarded from the fields to the towns and harbors for export to the West. Railroad building started everywhere, and rail length increased dramatically in all of East-Central Europe with the help of Austrian, British, German, and French capital. By the outbreak of World War I, the Hungarian railroad system had already reached the level of Great Britain in proportion to its population.

In connection with railroad building, western capital was instrumental in starting coal mining and iron production. A machine industry sprang up to produce rolling stock and agricultural machinery. In Hungary, a sugar industry was founded with Austrian capital, and 96 percent of the Rumanian oil industry was in German, British, and Dutch hands. Around 1900, 60 percent of the Hungarian and 92 percent of the Rumanian manufacturing industry was owned by foreigners.

The vast number of foreign loans and investments could not be handled without the creation of a banking system. In the decades around the turn of the century, a network of financial institutions sprang up in the region. The majority of the big Hungarian banks—or rather, of the big banks in Hungary—were owned by foreigners, in this case, by Austrian and, increasingly, by German groups. In Rumania, all eight leading banks were founded completely or partly by foreign, mostly German, capital.

The influence of foreign capital in Serbia and Bulgaria stood in sharp contrast to the core of East-Central Europe, even to the third Balkan state, Rumania. Foreign capital hardly promoted development toward capitalism. The small-scale subsistence level of the peasant economy did not attract western investors. Instead of foreign investments in the private sector, the governments received primarily state loans which were used above all to expand the bureaucracy and the military.

Export of western capital to the Balkans began during the 1860s and 1870s with the construction of a railway system. However, here it did not function as an impetus for industrialization and modernization, but served mainly foreign strategic-political aims—the connection of the West with the Near and Middle East. British and Austrian capital was initially involved, but it was soon overshadowed by the French and the Germans with their clashing imperialist aspirations in the area and beyond.

Foreign loans imposed such hard conditions that Serbia soon plunged into bankruptcy and could recover only with new western credits, which gave foreign powers, above all France, a tighter control of the economy and a prominent role in Serbian politics. Copper and coal mines were founded by the French; iron works, chromium, lead and zinc mining by the British; and sugar factories by the Austrians and the Germans. However, the significance of those direct investments was minor; they amounted to only 3 percent of government loans.

There was a similar situation in Bulgaria, for here also the main destination of foreign credit was the national debt. Interest payments swallowed up one-third of the public revenues and drove this country to the brink of bankruptcy. The ratio of productive foreign investments in Bulgarian enterprises was somewhat higher than in Serbia—5 percent—but as the amount was considerably lower, the role of promoting the country's economy was negligible.

The banking systems of Serbia and Bulgaria were also founded by foreign capital; however, they did not produce a network of financial institutions and failed to become an integral part of the economy. With the extremely low domestic capital accumulation, they were unable to supersede the typical medieval forms of credit and usury.

Foreign capital outlay, before World War I, in the Balkan Peninsula, exhibited strongly colonial traits. The investments did not lift the economy from an underdeveloped preindustrial, even pastoral level.

In the interwar period, the whole of East-Central Europe became "Balkanized" for foreign capital. Not only did its share sink below prewar level, but its distribution took on a distinct political character. In the core countries of East-Central Europe—Hungary, Poland, and Rumania—foreign capital had a 50 to 70 percent share during the postwar decades, but only about one-fifth was actually used for productive investments. The bulk of it served the reconstruction of the region where the ravages of the war and the disruptions caused by the disintegration of the Habsburg and

Ottoman empires drove all the countries to the brink of economic collapse, sociopolitical unrest, and instability.

One purpose of the loans was to avert a revolutionary situation in East-Central Europe by promoting financial recovery and building a "cordon sanitaire" to block any ideological contamination emanating from the Soviet Union. A new political alliance system had to be financed, mainly by France and the Little Entente, to encircle Hungary and forestall its menacing pressure for a revision of the unjust peace treaty that dismembered the country.

Credits came above all from France, Britain, and the United States, many in the form of League of Nations packages. In view of the chiefly political nature of the foreign credit operations, western financial activities showed no vivid interest in possible investments in the economies of the region. The only partial exception was the newly restored Polish state. In 1920, it was in a similar situation as the other countries of the region, fifty to seventy years earlier. Western capital, mostly French and to a lesser degree German and Belgian, found here a hitherto closed field in which to invest; it was economically, as well as politically, profitable. Two-thirds of Poland's metal and mining industry, 90 percent of its oil industry, half of the gas and waterworks, the chemical industry, and electrification and telecommunication fell into foreign hands. The capital-hungry new country, devastated by six years of war, was in desperate need of industrialization, but it lacked any significant domestic savings to begin the transformation from a poverty-stricken agricultural to a mixed agrarian-industrial structure.

In Hungary, as in the other countries of the region, only a small fraction of the very extensive foreign capital influx was spent to enhance modernization and productivity. Most of the economically productive investment went into electrification, transport, and telecommunication. The modest domestic accumulation, initiated by the prewar loans, now had to cover three-quarters of the capital invested in the economy, thus perpetuating its backwardness.

Rumania tried initially to minimize its dependency on foreign capital and follow an economic policy of self-reliance, but soon found it unworkable and ended the interwar period as the most indebted country of the region. Though nationalism reduced somewhat the foreign share, three-fourths of the oil industry, a considerable part in the metallurgic, cellulose, and paper industries, textile, cement, and building material factories remained in western, mainly French and British, hands.

In Yugoslavia, western capital controlled the majority in sectors of special importance for the investing countries, as in mining, electric power generation, the chemical industry, and communications. The overall share of foreign capital did not surpass, however, a quarter of the total investments. The modest foreign interest contributed to the fact that industrial development of interwar Yugoslavia grew only at a very slow pace, from 20 percent in 1920 to 21 percent in 1938.

In Bulgaria, the even more pronounced backwardness did not attract any significant foreign capital for productive investments. The only exception was the food industry because of its relative importance for the West. The other branches were left practically untouched. However, also in the interwar period, close to a third of banking capital remained under the control of foreign groups. Lack of western capital influx, together with the insufficient domestic accumulation, left Bulgaria a preponderantly agrarian country. About 80 percent of the population lived off the land, and capitalist structures emerged only as scattered islands in a sea of a primitive peasant economy and a rural way of life.

The outbreak of the world economic crisis, in 1929, changed the picture completely. Up to the end of the 1920s, modern capitalist development in East-Central Europe was still strongly influenced by foreign capital, even if its share showed a diminishing tendency and sank below the World War I level. Now, western loans nearly stopped; the capital export of the two biggest creditors dropped from $1.4 billion in 1930 to $300 million in just one year, then to $30 million two years later. While the Great Depression also dealt a heavy blow to the leading western powers, the countries of the east-central region were particularly hard hit. Mostly agrarian or agrarian-industrial, they were not only shaken, but attacked at the very core. Already deeply in debt, they again faced bankruptcy.

Suddenly deprived of foreign loans and investments which had, until then, for want of sufficient domestic capital accumulation, enabled East-Central Europe to surpass somewhat the prewar level, the countries of the region switched once again from a "western" to an "eastern" structural pattern. As the solution could not come either from abroad, or from the inner free market capitalist mechanisms, they tried to find a way out of the crisis with a five hundred–year-old regional response from above: the intervention of an authoritarian state. Foreign capital, as a substitute for the lacking domestic accumulation, was itself substituted by the state.

In the beginning of this chapter, we mentioned the triggering role of railway building in the structural transformation of the region. From the mid–nineteenth century on, the development of a modern transportation system was a joint enterprise of the state and foreign capital. Powerful international syndicates loaned capital to the state, and the state, as a very junior partner, granted them concessions and guaranteed 5 to 10 percent interest on the invested capital, on a scale and scope unknown in the West.

The other, perhaps the most typically regional form of state activity, was its direct intervention in the promotion of industrialization by legislation. Already in the last decades of the century, exemptions from taxation and from custom duties were granted; interest-free loans and state subsidies were introduced. State capital, mostly of foreign origin, went above all to branches serving the capitalist transformation, the founding, development, and enlargement of the textile, machine, iron, and chemical industries. While the customs union within the Habsburg Empire made it impossible for Hungary to apply protective tariffs at its own borders, the Bulgarian, Serbian, and Rumanian governments methodically fostered domestic industry through a combination of tariff policies and laws.

Although before World War I, the industry-supporting measures of the governments in the region did not exceed modest limits, they nevertheless marked the beginnings of the growing role of the state in breaking out of backwardness and dependency. Its direct effect on industrialization might seem limited, but much more important was the indirect influence it exerted on attracting foreign capital with favorable conditions and reassuring guarantees. Backwardness and dependency could not, of course, be counterbalanced by the economic activity of the state alone, but its intervention was instrumental in mobilizing and procuring the necessary sources of foreign capital at the start of the structural transformation of East-Central Europe. This foreshadowed its increasingly dominant role in the interwar period.

World War I created not only a new map of East-Central Europe, but also a political atmosphere laden with clashing interests. Victors such as the reestablished Poland, the new Czechoslovakia and Yugoslavia, and the vastly increased Rumania wanted to keep their gains; the losers, Bulgaria and Hungary, demanded revision of the unjust peace treaties. The growing nationalistic passions led to a powerful expansion of the state role in every aspect of social, political, economic, and ideological life. Nationalism became the dominant trend in influencing developing in the reshaped region.

Each state had to build a new organization out of the multiple segments of its new territory. Previous financial and economic ties were severed and new contacts had to be formed, and transportation systems had to be reoriented. Systematic encouragement of domestic industry with subsidies, tax exemptions, bonuses, high tariffs, import controls, and similar inducements were implemented on a far larger scale than ever before. The inflamed nationalism created new international tensions and led to a state-sponsored overt and covert build-up of an army and an armament industry. The center of protectionist policies shifted from light to heavy industries, from the haphazard dispersion in the prewar period along transportation routes and mineral sites to strategically oriented locations in a semiplanned and cartelized manner.

State intervention was necessarily furthered by the double change in the role of foreign capital. On the one hand, its direction had been shifted, as mentioned previously, from productive private investments to politically motivated state loans in order to avert financial collapse and social disturbances in the central European region. On the other hand, the nationalist-autarchic trend of self-reliance, concomitant to the militarization of the society, deliberately stemmed further foreign economic penetration and favored the development of domestic forces.

During the 1920s, custom tariffs to protect domestic industries from foreign imports were raised considerably and reached 30 to 50 percent in Hungary and Rumania, even 67 percent in Poland. The Yugoslav state introduced tariffs from 70 to 170 percent for industrial consumer goods. In Bulgaria, prewar duty rates doubled and trebled, erecting a prohibitive barrier in every field of domestic industry. State efforts took on not only a vastly increased protective character, but also the state sector itself expanded in the two victorious countries of the region. Both Yugoslavia and Rumania nationalized investments and properties of their former enemies— Germany, Austria, and Hungary; Rumania, from the start anti-Semitic, went further and grabbed "alien," that is, Jewish, shares by pressure or blackmail.

In Poland, after four years as a battleground, followed by two years of war with Soviet Russia, the devastation was especially disastrous, and state intervention was vital from the beginning. The nation entered independence without accumulating any domestic capital to speak of, and with hardly any industry. It ended independence at the outbreak of World War II with two-thirds of its population still making a living from agricultural endeavors, but only one-third of its national income deriving from it. The pressing necessity to force industrialization was achieved, besides the considerable foreign capital influx, by the dominant role of the state. Poland became the most striking example of state capitalism in the region. The state owned, among others, about one hundred industrial companies with more than a thousand establishments. The armament industry was entirely state owned, 80 percent of the chemical, 40 percent of the iron, and half the metallurgical industries were in its hand. It held the majority of the stocks in fifty corporations, owned 20 percent of the oil refineries, and controlled, directly or indirectly, the Polish banking system.

In 1936, Poland started the implementation of a ten-year state plan to accelerate industrialization. Mainly for military reasons, a new Central Industrial District was to be created to concentrate armament and related plants away from the frontiers. Besides military installations, the state planned to build roads and railways, hydroelectric stations, and iron foundries. Many of the new installations were to be entirely state properties, but some mixed partnerships between the state and private industrialists were also foreseen, receiving tax exemptions, special state credits, grants, and privileges. The creation of this district is an outstanding example of the economic trend in the region to force industrialization with state planning, guidance, and interference within the limits of a controlled free market, with the aim of breaking out of backwardness and dependency. The results of the Polish experiment were beginning to show, with a rise of industrial production by 33 percent in three years, when the project was cut short by the joint German-Russian invasion in September 1939.

In contrast to Poland, Rumania began independence with only limited amounts of western aid to begin the transition from a semi-Asiatic feudal, even pastoral, structure to modern capitalism. Most of the western capital influx served the political interests of the great powers or represented speculative investments. A considerable part of foreign credits were wasted on utterly unproductive projects such as an inflated bureaucracy and military.

The role of the new state in the development of the banking system was overwhelming, even before World War I. Rumania was the first country in East-Central Europe to establish an elaborate system of both tariffs and laws favoring her nascent industry with tax reliefs, exemptions from customs duties, reductions of freight rates, preferences in orders, and allocation of state land for industrial buildings.

"Rumanization," an antiforeigner, anti-Semitic ideology, became the motor for the development toward state capitalism. The newly independent country established its state-owned financial institutions alongside the first entry of foreign banks and obliged industry and trade to impose fixed quotas to replace foreign and Jewish personnel with members of the ethnic majority. This policy laid the foundation of a highly bureaucratized, militaristic, xenophobic state, but hardly put a dent in its structural backwardness. By 1914, the number of industrial workers grew tenfold, but reached only 3 percent of the labor force; 81 percent of the population was involved in agriculture. Per capita, income in Rumania was the lowest in Europe, except for Serbia and Albania.

In the interwar period, state intervention grew much more pervasive. The government took over considerable industrial and financial assets invested by former enemy countries, above all, Hungary, which lost to Rumania the relatively industrialized, mineral-rich area of Transylvania. Not even the capital of western war allies was spared. In the oil industry, a vital branch of the economy, the Rumanian share grew from 6 to 27 percent, and concessions for exploitation of state-owned land were given only to Rumanians. A chauvinistic campaign of intimidation and black-mail was launched to purge enterprises from Jewish and foreign influences, and western capital was barred from investing in state-controlled mining and in new oil exploration. In 1925, the state seized all foreign credit balances and decided to achieve financial stabilization without any western loans under the slogan "Through Our Own Means." Foreign loans were reduced from about $670 million in 1914 to $320 million by 1929, before the onset of the great world depression. This placed the country at the bottom of the debtors' list in the East-Central European region.

The world economic crisis caused a setback to the politics of nationalization and self-sufficiency. The government was forced to cancel its antiforeigner mining laws and to ask for western loans; Rumania jumped from the bottom to the top of the foreign debt list. But even at the low point of the crisis, state intervention con-tinued its path toward domination. In the late 1930s state-controlled and sponsored cartelization encompassed nearly half of the total industrial capital, in metallurgy as much as 90 percent. Toward the end of the decade, a Superior Economic Council was established. It drew up national planning directives for industrial concentration, additional capital nationalization, manpower allo-cation, price and consumption regulation. The introduction of comprehensive state planning was on its way when growing pres-sure from Nazi Germany changed the course of Rumania's political and economic situation. It included the country first in the German *Grossraumwirtschaft* and soon in Hitler's war machine.

The overall results of state intervention were, however, much less impressive than theories and laws indicated. In the interwar de-cades, the industrial share of the national income grew only from 24.2 to 28.4, that is, by 17 percent; the agrarian population re-mained constant at 80 percent; and average per capital national income grew from $50 to just $81—this at the same time that it reached $300 to $440 in western Europe.

The effect of state intervention was counterbalanced by the per-sistent heritage of Turkish-type feudalism: insufficient capital ac-cumulation, rampant graft, squander and incompetence of the new "ethnic" bourgeoisie, and the patronage system of a corrupt bu-reaucratic state oligarchy. In addition to this came the restrictions on western capitalists and Jewish entrepreneurs, neither of which the weak autochthonous middle class was capable of replacing. All these factors constituted an insurmountable brake on development. The chauvinistic slogan "Through Our Own Means" remained illusory. Rumania's socioeconomic structure stayed at the bottom of the backward East-Central European region.

In the other two Balkan nations, Yugoslavia and Bulgaria, the role of the state in the capitalist transformation of their socioeconomic structures differed significantly from that in Rumania.

The beginnings were very similar. All three nations gained independence in the last quarter of the nineteenth century. Their structures were preponderantly agricultural, neither had any previous domestic capital accumulated. In trying to shed the legacy of Turkish-type feudalism, all were in need of foreign capital and all attempted to break out of backwardness and dependency through state intervention. None succeeded. At the start of World War II, they remained underdeveloped and agrarian, at the bottom of a backward region.

State measures to promote and shelter domestic industrialization in Serbia and Bulgaria were similar to those described in the Rumanian development: protective laws, high tariffs, tax exemptions, duty concessions, subsidies, and so forth. Their impact was minimal. Until 1906, the trade agreement with the Habsburg Empire allowed free import into Serbia of all goods not produced in the country, that is to say, nearly all industrial products. On the eve of World War I, the total invested capital in Serbian industry was about $12 million; more than half of it from foreign sources—quite trivial amounts in view of the $200 million foreign, mostly government credits, three-quarters of which served strategic and political purposes, and most of the remaining quarter controlled the rich mineral resources.

The economist H. Feis wrote sarcastically but pertinently: "When the new Serbian state first opened the eyes, its gaze fell on the creditors surrounding its cradle" (quoted in Berend and Ranki 1974, 107; this chapter closely follows their standard work). This was true also for the adolescent Yugoslavia. In the interwar years, it still concentrated on foreign capital as the basis for industrial development. About 60 percent of industrial investments and more than 75 percent in mining was in western hands. The state share grew considerably, mainly by taking over previous Austrian, Hungarian, and German investments, but it remained inadequate. In the decisive years of the 1920s, the state was partly unable, partly unwilling, to break the preponderant, mostly politically inspired western influence.

With the onset of the world economic crisis, more stringent measures were introduced to encourage domestic industrial development. However, state intervention came much too late; it could not change Yugoslavia's semicolonial status. Despite rich mineral resources, only 2 percent of the national income in 1939 derived from this source. The country remained preponderantly agricultural; the share of the peasant population diminished only insignificantly—from 77 to 76 percent; that of industry grew by just 10 percent in the twenty years between 1920 and 1940; per capita income reached less than a quarter of the average western level.

Bulgaria's passage from archaic feudalism into the industrial-capitalist age was even less successful. For western capital, the development of its small peasant economy did not seem more attractive after the war. The Bulgarian national debt, at the end of the interwar period, amounted to only $150 million, the smallest in the region, and half of this insignificant amount derived from the prewar years.

In view of the negligible domestic accumulation and equally negligible foreign capital influx, the state had to fill the role of protecting and promoting industrial development. It issued a series of comprehensive laws to encourage growth. New industrial ventures received gratuitous cessions of state-owned land, substantial reductions of freight charges, tax and customs exemptions, and other advantages. In the twenty interwar years, industrial output increased five- to sixfold.

This growth is impressive, but at the same time, misleading. In the official statistics, on the eve of World War II, industry employed 280,000 persons, but most were occupied in handicraft enterprises, so that the number of factory workers, in the western European sense of the word, was no more than 45,000—only 3 percent of the economically active population.

The growth is even more misleading if we consider the general socioeconomic structure of the country. The agrarian population diminished only from 80 to 78 percent; one-third of the peasants owned less than 5 hectares and lived at mere subsistence levels; only 1.6 percent owned more than 100 hectares with possibilities for capital accumulation to stimulate industrialization. In the mid-1930s, wooden plows were still more numerous than iron ones.

Ironically, state support helped not only growth, but also the perpetuation of backwardness. Typical industries for starting the Industrial Revolution in the West—the iron, machine, metal and chemical industries—showed no advance in interwar Bulgaria; their combined relation to total output even diminished from 10 to 8 percent. The one apparent exception was energy, which showed an increase from 3 to 12 percent, but it was also the only branch where foreign, mainly Belgian, capital played a decisive role. On the other hand, the share of the old traditional pottery more than doubled and that of the textile industry grew from a quarter to a third of the total. The latter is especially telling, as this branch generally played a diminishing role in the western spurt of industrialization. To round out the picture, productivity per worker in the leading industrial sectors remained virtually constant in the interwar period.

Growth of state-encouraged industry *and* continued structural backwardness has its explanation in specifically Bulgarian politics. None of the interwar governments, whether leftist-populist or rightist-authoritarian, could afford to place major burdens, necessarily involved in modern industrialization, upon the huge majority of small peasants. The immediate economic interest of the peasants, but also their whole system of social values, clinging to equality and tradition, opposed large-scale enterprises and modernization, as well as foreign capital intrusion. Militant irredenta and nationalism further strengthened the peasants' aversion to modern transformation and tied even tighter the hands of the state to intervene in favor of any radical socioeconomic structural change. Bulgaria started its road to capitalism at the very bottom of the region and remained there at the end of the road, in 1944.

In Hungary, etatism constituted a basic ideological tenet of all interwar governments. The state was to be powerful, even supreme, the bearer and upholder of nationalism and independence. In economic policy, however, state interference remained a limited, indirect one until the Great Crisis of the 1930s. Although the state sector increased in this subperiod, from one-fifth to one-quarter of the gross national product, growth was due mainly to the development of an unproductive, oversized state apparatus and bureaucracy. In accordance with the prevailing policy of economic isolationism and protectionism, the state tried to enhance the rapid development of the domestic industry as the pillar of a sheltered, independent internal market, in order to overcome the one-sided agrarian structure of the country. Free from the constraints of the prewar Austro-Hungarian customs union, the state introduced and radically raised protective tariffs to 50, even 75 percent for light industrial, above all textile products, while the rates on heavy industrial products and certain raw materials remained moderate, or even free from import duties. The magnitude of this isolationist policy is well illustrated by the fact that, in the mid-1920s, the customs tariff list contained rates for 2,244 articles.

State intervention played a decisive role in the progress of industrialization. During the subperiod of 1920–1929, the production index rose from 100 to 294, the number of factory workers nearly doubled, and the share of industry in the gross national product increased by 30 percent, from one-fifth to one-third. Even this rapid rise could not change the relative backwardness of Hungary. Its industrial production per capita was still less than a quarter of the average in the developed west.

In the field of agriculture, a kind of "negative state intervention" was practiced. The state intervened against pressure from big landowners to pursue an agrarian capitalism, where banking and industry was just a complement, an appendage of agrarian interests. At the same time it intervened, even with its police power, against the demands of the land hungry peasantry to carve up huge semifeudal estates. The state consciously chose industrial protectionism and left agriculture to fend for itself. It kept the peasants as citizens in name only, cannon fodder in the battle for industrialization.

But the state did not abandon the big landowners. Contrary to other countries in the region, it essentially preserved the semifeudal system of large estates. Over half the population remained occupied in agriculture, its share in the national income diminished by 13 percent, while the industrial share increased by 20 percent.

The great world economic crisis completely changed the picture, and with it, the role of the state. The agricultural economy collapsed; the price of cereals dropped to a third, even to a fifth its earlier price; export volume fell by 50, its value by 70 percent; production was nearly halved; and small holders, as well as big landowners, ran out of cash and credit, and lapsed into a kind of self-sufficiency.

The crisis forced the state to reverse its hands-off policy. State support for produce marketing grew fifteenfold, debts were lowered, transportation costs diminished, export became considerably monopolized, subsidies were introduced to improve product quality, and prices for industrial items for agricultural use reduced. Central price control was established, and a bonus system was created to support exporters.

This bonus system was also applied to industrial products in order to reduce imports and increase exports. It became part of a new fiscal policy that placed foreign trade under total state control and radically changed its composition. The share of industrial finished goods in imports was cut in half while that of raw materials and semimanufactured products grew to a third of total imports. The change was especially dramatic in the textile industry. In 1928, before the onset of the crisis, 30 to 45 percent of consumption was imported; by 1935, it had dropped to 2 to 3 percent. State control was also responsible for the shifts in industrial exports. The radically diminished share of the food industry was taken over by textile and heavy industrial products.

Thus, in the crisis years, state intervention became an indispensable tool of recovery. By the mid-1930s, agrarian production increased by 20 percent, export value by 50 percent, though both still lagged behind the peak level of 1928. Even industrial production fully recovered from its 24 percent fall in just four years, faster than in most developed western countries.

After 1938, state intervention became complete as Hungary was, step-by-step, integrated first into Hitler's *Grossraumwirtschaft*, later into German rearmament, and finally into its war machine. An ever increasing part of the economy worked upon state orders, and financing passed into the hands of the state. Rationing of food and industrial products was introduced; compulsory delivery to the state with fixed quotas was ordered for agrarian produce and livestock; prices were regulated at fixed levels; and additional state bureaucracy was created to direct and control the economy.

In the five years from 1938 to 1943, the structure of the Hungarian economy changed dramatically: industrial production rose by 62 percent. For the first time in Hungarian history, the share of the peasant population sank below 50 percent, and industry produced a larger part of the national income than did agriculture. At the same time, the structure of the economy was not only changed, but also distorted, as the developments did not arise from internal pressures to break the one-sided agrarian, backward character of the country, but from outside pressure to prepare and conduct a war in the service of German military needs.

By the end of 1943, the war-induced, state-driven boom suddenly stopped. Stagnation, then decline, set in. With the occupation of the country, in March 1944, any tentative independent political and economic effort had to cease. Open German plunder and exploitation began its work of destruction, which became total after October 1944 with the power seizure and terror of the fascist Arrowcross movement amidst the ravages of war in the wake of the advancing Red Army.

In contrast to Hungary, Nazi Germany considered Rumania from the beginning to the end as an agricultural and raw materials colony. The German grip on the country was overwhelming, aided by the subservience of the right-wing military dictatorship. Germany became practically the sole market for its agrarian products, and any growth of industry was discouraged. In the conflicting interests of an interventionist state and Germany's veto to developing, or just maintaining, Rumanian industry as such, the latter proved much stronger. Even a request for help to build up a modern armament industry was brusquely rejected, and Rumania, Hitler's most enthusiastic ally in the war against the Soviet Union, remained fully dependent on Germany and German-controlled Czech armaments. The country's rather limited heavy industry was penetrated and ultimately controlled by German enterprises. In oil production, of paramount strategic importance for warfare, Germany increased its interest from less than 1 percent in 1939 to 47 percent in 1941.

The war hardly changed anything in the socioeconomic structure of Rumania. No efforts were made to raise the productivity of its backward agriculture which, in contrast to Hungary, had to struggle without any state support. The forced cereal export to Germany (1.4 million tons between 1940 and 1944 versus Hungary's 100,000 tons) soon led not only to rationing of consumption, but to outright agreements stipulating that after the satisfaction of German requirements, only the leftovers could be diverted to cover the needs of the population. The only exception in the stagnating industrial production was the heavy industry under German control, but even here, the increase of 30 percent was achieved by overutilization of the existing capacity. Oil production was kept steady for a long time, but dropped in 1944 to half its prewar level, due to the heavy Allied air strikes. The country entered the postwar world with a still predominantly agricultural structure, its exhausted industrial plants and production resources in very poor condition, and its oil wells badly damaged. However, the last minute pull-out of Hitler's war with the Soviet army at its frontiers, spared Rumania the same catastrophic destruction suffered by neighboring Hungary and Yugoslavia.

The fascist Slovak puppet state profited considerably from Germany's plan to expand its war production. Total industrial output increased by 60 percent, from 1938 to 1943. The war boom carried along with it every branch, even the production of consumer goods. The net effect was a rapid industrialization in a country which, at the time of the dismemberment of Czechoslovakia, had very little industry to add to its agriculture and forestry. Notwithstanding the relative unimportance of small, mountainous Slovakia, the structural changes became significant for the postwar integration of the restored Czechoslovakia into the Soviet bloc.

Much less important for the German war effort was its southernmost Balkan ally, Bulgaria. Its backward, small, peasant economy could contribute hardly anything. As a source of raw materials and industrial goods, even as a grain exporter, it remained negligible, and the war left the underdeveloped structure of the country unchanged. On the contrary, by the end of the war, grain production fell to 77 percent of its prewar level, its exports to Germany fell from 200,000 to 50,000 tons. Industrial production of consumer goods stagnated or decreased, and it diminished even in heavy industry, the only branch the Axis powers would have been interested in.

Following its pro-Russian tradition, Bulgaria succeeded in avoiding participation in the aggression against the Soviet Union, though eager enough to join in the German attack on Yugoslavia and Greece. It was rewarded by Hitler with a chunk of both countries, even with a part of Rumania to strengthen the political orientation of the pro-German royal-military dictatorship.

The shaky alliance broke down as soon as the Red Army neared its frontier. Bulgaria changed sides and declared war on Germany. Its army joined Tito's partisans in the liberation of Yugoslavia. Bulgaria, Hitler's latest ally, became the first ally of the Soviet Union among the former satellite countries. Under combined Soviet and popular pressure, its Communist-influenced Fatherland Front government began, again as first among the former satellites, its shortened, rapid road into the Soviet orbit.

Poland and Yugoslavia suffered the worst destruction. Both were attacked and occupied by Germany, their economies plundered, exploited to the utmost or wantonly destroyed, their populations reduced to the level of starvation. Poland's human losses were horrendous, more than 6 million out of a total of 32 million inhabitants. Besides the 300,000 soldiers killed, every fifth civilian Pole was murdered—among them, close to 3 million Jews. Additionally, 1.3 million were dragged from their homes and used as slave laborers in German factories.

The dismembered Yugoslavia lost 1.8 million persons, 12 percent of its population; about half were killed by the Germans, the other half died in the civil war, with Tito's partisans against the German-equipped Croatian army, the Serb anti-Communist Cetniks, and the royalist underground forces. In Croatia, the German-Italian puppet state, the fascist Ustasha slaughtered 350,000 Serb men, women, and children, and exterminated the majority of Jews. The German plunder of grain, foodstuffs, and raw materials was as ruthless as in Poland, not just in the occupied territories, but also in "independent" Croatia, the economy of which was disrupted by the severed links to Serbia. Its total oil production served the German war machine, and close to half of its forests had to be cleared to satisfy the German need for timber. By 1944, a third of Croatian territory was in the hands of Tito's partisans and was used as a base to liberate all Croatia from the Ustasha regime and its German masters.

6

Anti-Semitism and the Holocaust

JEWS IN A DIVIDED EUROPE

This chapter departs in many respects from the structure of the book. It centers on a single social factor, anti-Semitism, and offers a rather detailed political narrative at its outcome. However, the basic differences between western and East-Central anti-Semitism and the Holocaust provide a striking and tragic illustration of the main subject of the book, the consequences of the separation of the two regions. It also fits to follow the previous chapter, for, as Istvan Deak aptly remarks in his excellent essay: "The history of the Right in Hungary between the two world wars is the whole chronicle of Hungary at that time, for between 1919 and 1944, Hungary was a rightist country" (Deak 1966, 364). We can add to his statement Poland and Rumania as well.

* * *

The five hundred–year division of Europe is strikingly evident in the differing history of anti-Semitism in the two regions. It determined decisively the fate of the Jews and put its distinctive stamp on the Holocaust. We can keep relatively short the well-known historical developments in the West, but it will be necessary to go into more details regarding East-Central Europe to highlight the basic differences.

As has been shown, the general crisis of European feudalism elicited two opposite responses: the West started toward a decomposition of feudal structures and ultimately a new social, economic, and political system; East-Central Europe toward an intensification of feudalism and ultimately a halfway western turn in a semiold, seminew distorted manner, in an unsuccessful attempt to break out of backwardness.

The consequences of the West-Central rupture are well defined in the theoretical model by Barrington Moore. In his analytical theory, the political outcome is dependent on the relationship of the main classes at the moment when a society has to confront the disintegration of the feudal and the emergence of the protoindustrial society. With the existence of a strong, independent urban-commercial class taking control of the state from below, as in England, the economic and, in France, the political revolution, the result will be democratic capitalism. If a strong bourgeoisie is lacking and the landed class sponsors the commercialization of agriculture and industry by a perverted "bourgeoisie revolution from above," and at the same time retains control of the state, a fascist type of system will emerge.

Anti-Semitism and Holocaust in the Western Region

The breakthrough in the transformation of the disintegrating feudal structures occurred in England in the seventeenth century. Parallel to, and as a result of it, came the emancipation of the Jews. After their readmission to the country in the same century, their gaining of equal rights went hand in hand with defeudalization. Early on, there were no significant restrictions: no ghetto system was enforced; violence against them was virtually unknown; even the slight disabilities were removed right after the Industrial Revolution. The anti-Semitic tirades of some Catholic intellectuals, like Hilaire Belloc, around 1900, remained without echo, and the fascist movements of the 1920s were theatrical and politically insignificant. Though the organization of Oswald Mosley gained some temporary influence in the crisis years of the 1930s, his Jew-baiting became a particularly fatal liability because it led to his being associated with Hitler, whose brand of anti-Semitism only a few eccentrics could stomach.

Holland and Belgium followed the English model, early urban development led to the factual emancipation of the Jews, and the occupation of the French revolutionary army had only to legalize their rights. Until the crisis years of the 1930s, Jewish equality was not threatened in either of these two countries.

In France, the precapitalist transformation of commerce and banking began in the seventeenth century. Jews played hardly any role in it; they had been expelled in 1306 and were readmitted only in scattered small groups from the sixteenth century on, living in semimedieval conditions. The conflict between the political framework of the tenacious feudal absolute monarchy and the rising new social forces culminated in the Revolution. It established the sociopolitical foundations of the bourgeois democracy and brought equal rights for the Jews.

At the peak of radiating power from the revolution, France governed large parts of the western continent. Its institutions and laws were automatically applied or were obvious models for the local administrations.

Paradoxically, France, the revolutionary pioneer of emancipation, also became the pioneer in the revival of western anti-Semitism. Jews here were catapulted suddenly into full equal rights, and a hundred years later, their social emancipation was not yet complete, as shown by the Dreyfus affair, when a Jew dared to intrude into the still almost solidly conservative-monarchist-Catholic higher ranks of the army.

Chauvinism, rightist Catholicism, and fear of the organized working class produced a multitude of insignificant and ephemeral anti-Jewish movements, founded mainly in the 1890s by intellectuals. The most prominent was the *Action Française*, founded by the writer Charles Maurras. Its impact, however, remained restricted to, though rather influential in, certain literary circles, a side show on the monarchist-intellectual periphery until the 1930s and 1940s, on the whole academic in character. Characteristically, in the excellent essay of Eugen Weber on the history of the French Right since the Revolution, anti-Semitism merits only a few short paragraphs in the forty-one pages covering this long period.

Anti-Semitism, however, did not remain academic in character. Its flare-up in the 1930s was due to the world economic crisis, the Communist threat to the weakened capitalist structures, and the triumph of German fascism infecting the continent with its Jew-hating propaganda.

Despite the catastrophic consequences of the crisis, the stable structures of the West proved to be, to a great extent, resistant to the anti-Semitic contagion. In France, the monarchist *Action Française* gained some strength. Its radical offshoot, the militaristic *Croix de feu*, was by far too weak to threaten the democratic order. Both movements were not strictly fascist; they lacked the support of the main conservative Right. Only the outright national socialist splinter groups of Marcel Déat and Jacques Doriot succeeded during the Munich crisis in combining the defeatist slogan, *Mourir pour Dantzig?* (To die for Danzig?) with *Mourir pour les Juifs?* (To die for the Jews?)

In Holland and Belgium, the French pattern was repeated with some variations. The Dutch Nazi movement began to gain influence in 1935 when it received 8 percent of the vote. But only two years later, its poll declined to 3.8 percent, and the next year, it faded into near extinction. In Belgium, the two fascist parties, the Rexists and the Flemish autonomists, received subventions from the German Nazi Party, as did their Dutch counterparts. After initial successes, the Rexist movement shrank to a mere 4 percent in the 1939 vote, and the Flemish fascists did not even participate in the election. At the threshold of war, both parties were politically dead.

In France, Holland, and Belgium, the pro-Nazi parties were resuscitated only by their German masters who lifted them to power as Hitler's agents in his crusading war against democracy, communism, and the Jews.

The western Holocaust is a living history, its tragic history need not be detailed. Under the occupation, a broad scale of collaboration ensued. The puppet authorities became tools of the occupiers, their police rounded up the Jews, herded them into transit camps, and handed them over to the Germans for deportation and extermination, while the "Aryan" population looked on in a more or less indifferent—even approving—silence. Organized resistance to save the Jews was absent until the defeat of the German army became self-evident. The only exception was the general strike of Dutch workers in February 1941, partly in protest to the prelude of mass deportation, the seizure of 400 Jews to be transported to the concentration camp. The deportation of 105,000—75 percent of the Dutch Jews—was later obediently assisted by the local police. (The extraordinary rescue of the Danish Jews from deportation with the help of the entire population, happened nine months after the surrender of the German army in Stalingrad.)

Only after Stalingrad, in 1943, did the Vichy authorities dare to inform the Germans that no French police would be allowed to participate in the deportation of French Jews. Until Stalingrad, the German military commander in Belgium exempted the "unreliable" local police to be involved in rounding up Jews. After the German debacle, due to the scarcity of Nazi manpower, he changed his mind and ordered Belgian police to assist in the capture of the remaining Jews of Antwerp and Brussels. The Belgian police refused to obey, threatened to withdraw all cooperation, and the Germans had to relent.

Killing resistance fighters was quite in order, but murdering Jews as such was delegated to the German authorities. One of the few notorious exceptions was Paul Touvier, the fascist commander of the Vichy militia in Lyon, who ordered the massacre of Jewish prisoners in retaliation for the assassination of the minister of interior.

Otherwise, the puppet authorities, the fascist satellite parties, and their paramilitary organizations, the "ordinary westerners" did not murder Jews; however, they lent an often eager hand to the Germans in sending more than half a million to their death, 40 percent of the Jewish population in the western region. They became more or less willing accomplices of Hitler to get rid of "their" Jews, but collaboration ended at the frontier. The "ordinary" westerner might have been happy to grab "abandoned" Jewish property or denounce to the local authorities Jews in hiding, but there were practically no spontaneous killings, no pogroms. Once the Jews were out of the country, the dirty job was left to the Germans.

Anti-Semitism in the East-Central Region

As we have mentioned, around the year 1500, the countries of the region chose the "Second Serfdom" as an answer to the general European crisis and thus prolonged feudalism for centuries. First the German Electorate of Brandenburg detached itself from the West. Poland, Bohemia, and Hungary followed within two decades and soon formed the main social structure of the Habsburg Empire. Agriculture was based on a brutalized forced labor, while the incipient urban economy withered away.

In the long period of Second Serfdom, a medieval type of anti-Semitism characterized the region until the nineteenth century in Hungary and Prussia, even deep into the twentieth in Poland and Rumania. Jews were prohibited from owning land, confined to a primitive trade and finance by the grace of the feudal rulers who could, at will, expel them from, or readmit them to, towns and villages. They were constantly threatened by bloody pogroms as defenseless scapegoats for feudal exploitation or on the pretext of ritual murder charges. At about the same time that Jews lived and prospered freely in England, Holland, and Belgium, tens of thousands were slaughtered in Poland in a peasant uprising, and in Hungary, thousands were murdered, as "Turkish agents," by Austrian soldiers at the recapture of Buda. A few years after the French Revolution, Jews were once again expelled from Pest. In Walachia, the nucleus of Rumania, more than a hundred were slaughtered in a ritual murder accusation, and in Galicia, the Habsburg booty of the partitioned Poland, Jews were killed in a medieval blood libel pogrom just one year after the Emancipation Act in France.

Galicia

In Galicia, after the partition, the situation of Polish Jews deteriorated, rather than improved. The Polish type of anti-Semitic pattern was adopted by Austria. Exorbitant taxes were levied, Jewish marriages restricted, poverty increased, and pogroms chased them out of villages and towns in a vicious circle. The Habsburgs kept the province agricultural to serve as a granary for the empire, with any industrialization stifled. The 1848 Vienna revolution bypassed Galicia. The emancipation of the Jews was granted by the Habsburg Monarchy in 1848 and sabotaged by the Polish nobility, and only some twenty years later did the feudal Diet reluctantly agree to grant them equal rights.

Formal emancipation notwithstanding, widespread peasant pogroms continued. Even around the turn of the century, Jews were killed in villages. World War I brought about a new series of pogroms. During the invasion of the Tsarist army, hundreds of Jews were murdered by Russian soldiers and Polish peasants. Later, they were killed by Poles for siding with the Austrians and by Ukrainians for siding with the Poles. At the war's end, the victorious counterattack of the new national Polish army assumed the job. In its wake, Jews were murdered not only as Russian, but also as Bolshevik, agents. As McCagg writes, "Poland was reborn in Galicia in 1918–19 to pogrom music" (203).

* * *

Though the history of the eastern region lies outside the scope of this chapter, some remarks are appropriate. The connection of anti-Semitism with neoserfdom is as obvious in that region as in its East-Central counterpart. The differences only accentuate this connection: anti-Semitism within feudal Russia's specific Tsarist autocratic-statist structures was much more a state affair than in the Polish fragmented feudal structures where the nobility dominated the state and profited from, protected, or oppressed "their" Jewish subjects. In the Russian eastern regional type, the nobles— even the Orthodox Church—were subordinated to the state. The establishment of the Pale of Settlement by Tsarist ukaz, the enlarging or narrowing of its borders, is a good example of this reversed supremacy.

* * *

In the reconstituted *interwar Poland*, vicious anti-Semitism was not simply a manifestation of only the extreme Right, but was respectable in the mainstream of national life and a foremost issue in political affairs. Jews were perceived as a foreign body in society, to be excluded and gotten rid of. The connection of anti-Semitism with the preceding feudal period is strikingly evident here: the heritage of the Galician-Russian past defined decisively the interwar years.

Poland

Poland was one of the most backward countries of Europe; its socioeconomic structure remained preponderantly agricultural and was dominated by less than half a percent of large semifeudal estates on one side, and 5 million landless peasants on the other. In the middle, 65 percent of all holdings were tiny parcels too small even to support a single family. Only in 1937 did industry reach the initial prewar level, and even that late, it produced less than a third of the national income. Poland's national product per capita was a fourth of the western countries.

Another aspect of this East-Central backwardness is the fact that a considerable part of the bourgeoisie was Jewish. The distorted capitalist era catapulted them from their feudal functions as "pariah" financiers and small traders into the new economic structures. Their rapid expansion was much assisted by the feudal disdain of any entrepreneurial activity, unworthy for a Polish gentleman. The Jewish share in crafts, commerce, and industry grew in the ten years after 1921, from 19 to 60 percent, though preponderantly in small shops, petty trade, crafts, and minor industrial enterprises still dominant in interwar Poland. In the evolving big industry, their influence remained largely negligible. About 80 percent of Polish Jews lived below the official poverty level.

In certain branches, however, their share was decisive. Even in the mid-1930s, when the fascist state was well on its way to ousting Jews from economic life, they owned 69 percent of the textile industry, 88 percent of the milling, fur, and garment industries, and 76 percent of the canned food industries. They controlled 90 to 100 percent of the exports in textiles, canned food, and grain, and half of the commercial enterprises. A quarter of the lawyers and more than half of the doctors came from their ranks.

The preponderance of Jews in these sectors, and their relatively high share of the overall population—3.3 million of 31.9 million—made them convenient scapegoats for all the ills of Poland. A decisive factor in pervasive Polish anti-Semitism was the continued medieval caste character of the unassimilated majority of the Jews, their Yiddish language, distinctive dress, and religious practices. As the sociologist Celia Heller writes in her standard work: "The Polish majority did not need to pin the Star of David on them . . . at least 80 percent of the Jews were recognizable to Poles" (Heller 1977, 69). They were perceived as outsiders, strangers, especially inferiors, to be feared and despised. Only a tenth or even less of the over 3 million Jews were assimilated among them, mostly intellectuals, artists, professionals, and members of the higher bourgeoisie. Even close to the war's beginning, just 12 percent of all Jews registered Polish as their native language. Assimilation, however, led to its own negative stamp—that of the ungodly Jew, enemy of Christian values, poisoner of Polish culture.

The stipulations of the Versailles Treaty of 1919, which demanded equal rights for Jews, was disregarded from the beginning. Anti-Semitism became the chief ideology of all the Polish governments. Even the relatively tolerant Pilsudski dictatorship had to cede to popular pressure and turn more and more to the Right. For all of them, the solution for all the problems was to free the country from the Jews.

First, the government took from them traditional staples of tobacco, salt, matches, and alcohol and then excluded them from the nationalized, industrial, and commercial establishments; licenses for Jewish artisans were denied and state banks blocked credit to Jewish firms. A boycott of Jewish businesses was first tolerated, then actively promoted. Jewish market stalls were destroyed and Christian customers were threatened.

The universities became hotbeds of anti-Semitism. Jews were segregated in special dormitories. An incessant agitation led to the proclamation of a "Jewless Day," soon to become "Jewless Weeks"; "Ghetto Benches" were introduced in the classrooms; Jewish students were beaten, chased out, even killed. To block Jewish entry to universities and colleges, first an "informal" quota system was established, then a stringent official Numerus Clausus enacted.

The Church was an important pillar of anti-Semitism in this overwhelmingly Catholic country, where a large portion of the population still believed in medieval ritual murder. Sermons and publications advocated the elimination of Jews from the life of Christian society. This reached a peak with the pastoral letter from the Primate of Poland, Cardinal Hlond. While condemning violence, he gave his blessing to the anti-Jewish campaigns in economic and cultural spheres:

Jews fight against the Catholic Church, they constitute the vanguard of atheism and Bolshevism. . . . Jewish influence upon morals is fatal, they are committing frauds, practicing usury and dealing in white slavery. . . . One does well to avoid Jewish stores and stalls in the market. (Heller 1977, 113)

In 1937, official anti-Semitism reached its climax in the Ideological Declaration of the military-fascist government. It stated the elimination of the Jews as its central program. But the population did not need encouragement. Two years earlier, spontaneous, organized, tolerated, then instigated pogroms erupted all over the country. Jews were beaten and killed, chased out of towns and villages, their homes pillaged and burnt, their shops destroyed. The pogrom wave lasted until the eve of the German attack.

The Ideological Declaration was followed by a plan to prepare the forced mass emigration of Jews, though the word "deportation" was avoided. The long search for a place where they could be transported continued without success. The doors of Palestine were closed; America hid behind a stringent quota; the government's request from the League of Nations to place colonies under Polish mandate was rejected; a commission was even sent to Madagascar, but returned disappointed. The Germans solved this problem: They got rid of Polish Jews in their land of birth, in the death camps of Oswiecim-Auschwitz, Chelmno, Belzec, Sobibor, Majdanek, and Treblinka.

Hungary

In contrast to Galicia, at the beginning of the nineteenth century, Habsburg Hungary was well on its way into the New Age with loans to promote capitalist transformation. The middle, and even a part of the upper feudal nobility, soon grasped the historically proven usefulness of Jewish entrepreneurial skills, pursuits undignified for any aristocrat, and began to demand the end of their exclusion. Jewish emancipation and assimilation could modernize the country and, at the same time, gain Hungarian majority in the multinational kingdom.

The national uprising of 1848–1849, led by the middle nobility, the gentry, was a distorted "bourgeois revolution from above," an effort to exchange Habsburg rule for a liberal etatism under their control. It liberated the peasants from serfdom, but it did not abolish the rule of the nobility, and it did not distribute the feudal estate or create a national bourgeoisie.

The emancipation of the Jews, enacted in the last days of the revolution, did not survive the war of independence, crushed by the joint Russian-Austrian armies. The Habsburg dynasty was restored, the Jews were collectively punished with a heavy ransom for their support of the "rebels," and their emancipation was declared illegal. It was reinstated only in 1867.

The support of the Jews by the nobility developed into a tacit, peculiar contract between the ruling aristocracy and the upper echelons of the Jewish bourgeoisie. The adaption of Jews to national and economic life took a decisive surge. By the end of the century 80 percent declared themselves Magyars. They owned more than half of the commercial enterprises and made up 85 percent of the directors and owners of financial institutions. Some 20 "grand" Jewish families controlled 90 percent of the modern banking system and industrial plants; one-third of agricultural businesses were directly or indirectly controlled by Jews. They became in essence "a feudal estate in disguise, a corporate entity within the main body of the nation, endowed with privileges commensurate to their social function, but barred from the levers of political power" (Janos 1982, 118). Even that last hurdle was surmounted by the beginning of the twentieth century, as Jews became ministers and other high officials, accompanied by a massive campaign of ennoblement and a rise of intermarriages with the aristocracy.

This overall rapid ascent was encouraged by the aristocratic governments that kept a tight hold on any emergency concerning anti-Semitic agitation within the political system. Below this protective surface the fire of feudal anti-Semitism was smouldering in peasant villages and among the mainly German middle classes in cities. It suddenly broke out in 1882 in the medieval type ritual murder accusation in Tiszaeszlár. In its wake violent pogroms erupted all over the countryside. In Budapest, only military force could subdue mobs plundering Jewish homes and shops, and university students, incited by Catholic priests, beat up Jews. The Church, one of the biggest feudal landlords, became the main force behind Jew-baiting, a vocal backer of the short-lived anti-Semitic parties, the instigator against the growing leftist groups where Jewish students and intellectuals began to play a significant role.

After the war was lost, Hungarian anti-Semitism reverted to the specific East-Central pattern. The violent turn was fanned by the disproportionate participation of Jews in the revolutions of 1918–1919, at least two-thirds of the leaders of the Hungarian Soviet Republic were Jewish. In the White Terror following the overthrow of the revolution, the new national army and semiprivate officers' detachments joined hands in bloody pogroms, when many thousands of Jews were beaten, raped, tortured, and murdered. The counterrevolutionary government introduced the Numerus Clausus Act, quotas to cut back university admission of Jews. It was the first such anti-Jewish legislation in modern Europe, a pioneering precursor of the racist Nuremberg Laws.

It was also the beginning of a politically significant anti-Semitism. The radical change had many causes. Tens of thousands of Magyar civil servants, teachers, and former officers poured back from the successor states into the truncated country. Together with the new intelligentsia, risen from the ranks of peasantry and Christian bourgeoisie, they felt that it was the Jew who stood in their way of finding a place within the diminished possibilities. For the gentry, the Magyarized Jews lost their usefulness in shrunken homogenous Hungary. They changed their demand for social reform into an increasingly racist "Ersatz"-reform to oust the Jews.

After the ebbing of the violent anti-Semitic wave, the prewar pattern of aristocratic-Jewish bourgeois cooperation returned for a short time. The provisions of the Numerus Clausus were quietly ignored, and Jews regained a certain degree of guarantee for economic security and prosperity. By the end of the 1920s, the Jewish share of total national wealth was varyingly estimated at 20 to 33 percent.

Even during the decade of this consolidation era, the internal arena was dominated by ultranationalist, racist, anti-Semitic forces. They took over at the onset of the great world economic crisis. The social tensions between the semifeudal rule of the aristocratic estate owners and a distorted capitalist society without democracy, without a strong "Christian-national" bourgeoisie, and 3 million landless peasants in the background, suddenly erupted in an increasingly radical anti-Semitic upsurge. The protective umbrella of the aristocracy was swept away, and Hungary once again reverted to the "normal" anti-Semitism of the East-Central European region.

Free rein was given to the Jew-baiting demagogy. Encouraged by closer links to Nazi Germany, formerly somewhat restrained anti-Semitism became more and more vocal in large segments of the population. The pent-up tensions exploded in the mid-1930s, as the radical Right entered the national socialist groups, mainly the Arrowcross Party. They mobilized the streets with antifeudal, anti-Semitic slogans, and organized pogroms in villages and at universities. After the *Anschluss* of Austria to the Reich, their violence became even bolder. To placate Hitler and to steal the thunder of the fascists, in 1938 the government introduced a "Jewish law." Using not yet racial criteria, it established quotas of 20 percent in selected occupations to squeeze Jews out of their strongholds in the economy and the free professions.

Such a halfhearted measure, however, did not appease the Arrowcross. Now it openly stated its goal of seizing power. In the election of 1939, it received one-fourth of the votes, not only in the traditionally anti-Semitic strata, but also in parts of the working class and of the peasantry, formerly reduced to silence by an open vote.

Immediately after the election, the government enacted the second Jewish law, now based on racial criteria, with the quotas reduced from 20 to 6 percent. This was followed by a third one, which forbade marriage between Jews and non-Jews, and took over the Nazi notion of "racial disgrace" by making sexual intercourse with a Jew a punishable offense.

After the outbreak of the war, for a while the government tried to maneuver between keeping the country's independence and, at the same time, placating the pressure of the German and its own outright fascists. The easiest way out of this dilemma was to start a Hungarian-type independent Holocaust, to sacrifice a selected small group of Hungarian Jews without Hungarian citizenship. The attempt ended with the destruction of 450,000 Jews.

Rumania

Walachia and Moldavia were, since the fifteenth century, part of the Ottoman Empire. Under the relatively tolerant Turkish-type of feudalism, the population could keep its Eastern Orthodox religion. The Church, however, was less tolerant toward the few Jews living in the two provinces and, in 1640, it banned all Christians from having any contact with them. A long chain of pogroms followed, accompanied by blood libels. The nineteenth century began in 1801 with a pogrom in Bucharest. The mob, incited by ritual murder rumors, robbed and burnt Jewish homes; 128 Jews were killed.

Growing Russian influence, parallel to the weakening of the Ottoman Empire, led to a mass immigration of Russian Jews and aggravated the situation. During a short Tsarist occupation, the Organic Statues in 1830 introduced a Russian-type Second Serfdom. They denied citizenship to Jews and declared them a separate, alien nation. The uprising for independence in 1848, inspired by the neighboring Hungarian revolution, was quickly suppressed by a joint Turkish-Russian intervention, and the Organic Statutes were restored. Jews were prohibited from owning land or settling in the countryside. Forced into the towns, their upper strata became a pariah protobourgeoisie, while the poverty-stricken masses remained peddlers, tailors, innkeepers, and other traditional craftsmen.

Anti-Semitic measures, the exclusion of Jews from the body of the nation, survived the creation of the united Rumanian state in 1859. In spite of the stipulation of the Paris Treaty to grant equal rights to Jews, their emancipation was refused. The "revolution from above" was replaced by the 1862 "reform from above," enforced by the boyar middle nobility. The new constitution proclaimed the abolition of serfdom, but actually increased the leverage of the big landowners and kept the "reformed" neofeudalism dominant until the end of World War I. It also proclaimed equal rights for Jews, but the emancipation was practically obstructed by a parliamentary modification, which made citizenship "dependent on each individual case." The result was that until 1900, only 919 Jews out of a total of 267,000 became citizens. The anti-Semitic laws continued. Jews were prohibited from selling alcoholic beverages and carrying on peddler trading, they were excluded from the craft guilds, and their children were banned from state schools. The nineteenth century ended with the foundation of the International Anti-Semitic Alliance in 1895 with its symbol of the swastika, long before Hitler reinvented it. It had its role in the peasant uprising, in 1907, where 2,300 Jews and their families fell victim to anti-Jewish incitement.

The history of interwar Greater Rumania followed the Polish pattern. The nationalistic slogan, "Rumania for the Rumanians" of all governments led directly to a state policy of rolling back Jews from the economic and cultural spheres. Only after an ultimatum by the Great Powers, in 1923, was the constitution modified to grant citizenship to all Jews. In the same year, the League for Christian National Defense was founded, from which a new leader emerged, Corneliu Zelea Codreanu. His violent anti-Semitic movement, Legion of the Archangel Michael, was imbued with a mythical, even messianistic Christianity, and his incitement against "Judeo-Bolshevism" found an increasing echo in broad segments of the population.

In a bitter race for anti-Semitic votes, governments were pushed further and further to the Right. To steal the thunder of the fascists, they tried to suppress Codreanu and his Legionary movement with every legal and illegal means, even with murder. Codreanu was arrested, then, on November 30, 1938, was dragged from his prison, was led to a deserted area, and was strangled to death. During this period, hundreds, and according to some sources, even more than a thousand, legionaries were killed by the pro-Nazi government, with the tacit permission of Hitler.

On the other hand, the government now co-opted fully the ultra-Right's anti-Semitism. It looked idly on while at the universities Jewish students were beaten up, barred from going into their classes, and thrown out of windows or down stairs. The mob could, with immunity, set synagogues on fire and burn Torahs on public squares. Paramilitary detachments of the governing party vandalized Jewish quarters and destroyed or looted Jewish property. A quota system was introduced at the universities, and a review of the citizenship law was ordered so that more than 200,000 Jews became stateless from a total of 760,000. Many lawyers, doctors, druggists, and architects were barred from practice; Jewish professors were removed from their positions; and the Jewish-influenced press was destroyed.

Measures for the "Rumanization" of all economic activities were introduced. Jewish business enterprises were seized without compensation; private firms were obliged to hire Rumanian employees and fire Jewish ones; and in government sectors, the railroads and other enterprises, Jews were simply thrown out into the street. However, all those measures remained somewhat ineffective due to the pervasive graft of the Rumanian administration, the weakness of the "national" bourgeoisie, and the autocratic rule of King Carol, who feared that total de-Judaization would lead to economic chaos. By the end of the 1930s, the Jewish share, 4 percent of the population, was still 25 percent in domestic and 40 percent in import-export trade, 25 to 55 percent in industry; only 13 percent of "native" Rumanians, but 68 percent of Jews, were engaged in industry and trade.

With the murder of Codreanu, the outright fascist advance was halted, but a new leadership left the bulk of the movement intact. In September 1940, a military coup forced the abdication of the king, and General Ion Antonescu proclaimed himself the *führer* of the National Legionary State and chief of the Legionary Party. To preserve its independence from the military, the legionary movement fought back. The next four months were a training period. In Ploesti, Jews were tortured for days, then shot; in the Braila pogrom, Jews were thrown into the Danube and drowned; similar "minor" atrocities happened in other towns and villages.

These were only the prologue for the three nights and days of the great pogrom in Bucharest in January 1941. The mob, led by legionaries, burned down Jewish homes and synagogues while shops were pillaged. Several thousand Jews were dragged to the legionary headquarters, which had been converted into torture centers. Many were killed, others committed suicide. Groups that were rounded-up were murdered in the woods. An especially barbarous mass killing took place in the city abattoir where more than a hundred men, women, and children were slaughtered, their bellies slashed with a butcher's knife, then hung on meat hooks. Later, the corpses were chopped up and displayed with the inscription "Kosher meat."

The legionary rampage in the Rumanian capital did not fit into the plans of the military dictatorship. It interfered also with the German plans to prepare for an orderly participation of Rumania in the impending attack on the Soviet Union. Rumanian military units were dispatched, and after a short resistance, the legionaries surrendered.

The East-Central European Holocaust

The historic division of Europe decisively influenced not only the character of anti-Semitism, but also that of the Holocaust. Genocide here was organized *and* spontaneous, a concerted slaughter perpetrated by the fascist governments *and* the population. Its brutal pogrom-type character differed fundamentally from the indirect complicity in the western region. Hitler's Germany doubtlessly triggered, inspired, helped, and encouraged the willingly committed "final solution," but it was the "ordinary" Rumanian, Hungarian, Slovak, Croat, Lithuanian—even Pole, as much as he could under the circumstances—whether in army, gendarmerie, police, paramilitary fascist uniform or without it, who willingly massacred his own Jews. This independent Holocaust ran parallel to, and in connection with, the German Holocaust.

The East-Central genocide was the climax in the 450 year-long varying history of oppression of Jews, due to centuries of feudalism prolonged and brutalized by the Second Serfdom, but also to the bogged down, distorted "bourgeois revolution from above," which gave birth to a deformed capitalism without a significant "native" bourgeoisie. The feudal heritage of religious anti-Semitism is evident in many symbols of East-Central fascism, as in Codreanu's Brotherhood of the Cross and the Legion of Archangel Michael, in the early Hungarian Brotherhood of the Scythe and the later Arrowcross Party, but also in the leading profascist role of the Church in Slovakia and Croatia. In the predominantly agrarian countries of the region, the image of the Jew as Christ-killer was still very much alive. The regional genocide was a homegrown product, but without Hitler's triumph, there would have been no Holocaust in the east-central region or anywhere else.

Under the historical circumstances created by Germany, the people of the East-Central region perpetrated their separate Holocaust. That they murdered "only" more than half a million Jews, as compared with 5.5 million by the Germans, was due to their unequal strength. They slaughtered as many Jews as they could put their hands on, in their own countries and in the small chunks of occupied territories that their limited power reached—the Hungarians in the "liberated" parts of Czechoslovakia, Yugoslavia, and Rumania, and the Rumanians in those of the Soviet Union. They share the guilt for the genocide in a proportion and on a scale given by their possibilities.

Rumania

On June 21, 1941, Rumania joined the attack on the Soviet Union, to regain Bessarabia and Bukovina, seized by the USSR a year before. The advance of the Rumanian army was accompanied by anti-Jewish pogroms and massacres of exceptional brutality. The territories were "liberated" of practically all their Jewish inhabitants. In village after village, in towns and cities, the first thing the Rumanians did was to assemble communists and Jews and murder them. We restrict ourselves to a very few examples, because of their extreme magnitude and barbarity. As soon as the Rumanian army entered Cernauti, the capital of Bukovina, in less than twenty four hours over two thousand Jews were killed on the spot by soldiers let loose by their commanders, by armed legionary bands, and by the local mob. In Chisinau, capital of Moldavia, more than ten thousand Jews were massacred in the first two days. When the army entered the Ukraine, the pogrom in the city of Moghilev claimed four thousand Jewish lives. After the conquest of Odessa, the commander of one of the quickly installed holding camps set stables on fire housing five thousand old and sick Jews and burnt them alive. The remaining forty-three thousand ablebodied Jews were sent to the nearby forest and shot. Two hundred were kept alive to pile up the corpses, the guards set the piles afire, then also shot the two hundred "helpers."

In the hinterland of the main army advance, the local mob took over the killings. The Rumanian military administration, in collaboration with local authorities, organized the deportation of the surviving Jews to Rumanian concentration camps in the occupied territories.

In September 1942, about half a year after the German death

camps in Poland had gone into operation, Hitler instructed Antonescu to deport Jews from Rumania proper to the extermination camps. Antonescu stalled, then refused. It had become obvious to him that the war would be lost. When in March 1944 the Red Army neared the "liberated" areas, the camps had to be evacuated to the home territories. More than 300,000 Rumanian Jews, 40 percent of their total number, died during their deportation, in the camps and by pogroms. To those we have to add the 150,000 Ukrainian Jews massacred during the Rumanian occupation. The Rumanians did not need German help; they did it all by themselves.

Hungary

Until the German occupation on March 19, 1944, Hungary was an exception among the East-Central European satellites. By that time, in Rumania, already 40 percent had been massacred or sent to death camps. In the puppet states of Slovakia and Croatia, in Serbia and in Poland, 80 to 95 percent of the Jews had been massacred or sent to death camps. In Hungary, enlarged by Hitler's grace with parts of Slovakia, Transylvania, and Yugoslavia, "only" 63,000 Jews were killed, 7.6 percent of a total of 825,000.

The reasons for this slow start were already mentioned: the cautious maneuvers of the conservative-rightist government to keep the independence of the country, but at the same time to placate Hitler and the domestic fascists; the historic connections between the Jewish high bourgeoisie and the aristocracy, tacitly still operational under Prime Minister Count Pál Teleki.

This preliminary phase of the Hungarian Holocaust started in July 1941 with the massacre of eighteen thousand Hungarian Jews living in the "liberated" Slovak territories. Hungarian gendarmes rounded them up and deported them to Kamenec-Podolsk, where a mixed Hungarian-German-Ukrainian force slaughtered all of them. This mass murder fit into the double-tracked policy of the rulers and even soothed their consciences as only Jews without Hungarian citizenship were sacrificed.

This was followed by the slaughter in and around the city of Ujvidék, "liberated" from partitioned Yugoslavia in January 1942. Hungarian soldiers, with the connivance of their commanders, rounded up over a thousand Jews—men, women, and children—

shot them into the Danube and pushed the resurfaced bodies with long-stemmed cudgels under the drift-ice so that no traces would be left.

Savage killings organized by the army from above, mixed with murderous brutality by "ordinary" guards from below also characterized the fate of Jewish conscripts in the forced-labor battalions shipped to the Russian front in 1942–1943. First, mass executions and inhumane conditions decimated them, then during the long retreat of the beaten Hungarian army, every day dozens of exhausted Jews were killed or left on the wayside to freeze to death. In Kiev, sick forced-laborers were separated in shacks that were then set on fire by the guards, with hundreds fleeing the flames slaughtered by machine guns. From the thirty-eight thousand Jewish conscripts, twenty thousand perished, not including the war casualties or those taken prisoner by the Russian army.

The next phase of the Hungarian Holocaust, after the German occupation on March 19, 1944, has a "western regional" character. On behalf of the Germans, Hungarian gendarmes and policemen concentrated all the Jews living in the provinces in ghettos, loaded them into cattle trains, and at the frontier handed them over to the Germans for deportation to the death camps.

The division of labor with German planning, Hungarian implementation, and German extermination corresponds to the "western" pattern, but with two East-Central differences. One was the enormous number of victims, nearly half a million; the total Jewish population in the Hungarian province had been deported within six weeks. The other difference was the extreme brutality with which the deeply anti-Semitic Hungarian gendarmerie carried out its part of the deportations. Even the Germans were shocked by the ruthlessness—shocked, but approvingly supportive. Only the Jews holed up in Budapest escaped, for the time being protected by the conservative-aristocratic puppet government, that sensed the inevitable German defeat.

The last phase of the Hungarian Holocaust in all its East-Central savagery started with the power seizure of the fascist Arrowcross Party on October 15, 1944, aimed at the destruction of the 230,000 Jews of Budapest. The pogrom began the first night, as fascist thugs beat Jews wherever they found them, rounded up and deported 76,000 during the six weeks at their disposal before the capital was encircled by the Red Army. Arrowcross paramilitary detachments led 50,000 Jewish forced-laborers in a death march to the German frontier. They were driven by foot in the icy winter; only 35,000 arrived, 15,000 were left on the roadside dying, beaten to death or shot en route.

In the encircled Budapest, Jews were seized on the streets, and the armed militia made them march to the outskirts to dig defense trenches. Dozens were shot on the way into the Danube because they did not march fast enough; others were gunned down into the open trenches because they did not dig fast enough. By December, the Jews were concentrated in ghettos. Everybody found on the streets or hidden in houses not marked by the Star of David was shot on the spot, or dragged into the Arrowcross headquarters, robbed and tortured, then shot into the icy Danube. Armed fascist bands went to hospitals looking for Jews, dragged patients out, and murdered them.

Special militia squads prepared for the liquidation of the ghettos; the date of the final solution was set for January 15. The order was only rescinded by the intervention of a German general who feared that the mass murder would interfere with the defense of Budapest. Anyhow, it was too late. On January 18, Pest was liberated by the Russians; in Buda the Arrowcross forces held out for another month, but their armed militia went on with the pogrom until the last day. Thanks to the liberation of Budapest, about half of the Jews in the capital survived.

Poland

The German attack brought a tragic end to Poland, as close to 3 million "subhuman" civilians were murdered by the Nazis, about the same number as Jews. Consequently, the Polish contribution to the Holocaust remained minimal, though significant in our context: victims themselves, they still victimized the Jews.

A few days after the German aggression, civilians began to plunder Jewish shops and homes. When German soldiers attacked Jews, people applauded and joined in the brutalities. Polish police and gendarmerie, militiamen and civil volunteers denounced hidden Jews to Germans. In 1942, when the evacuation from the ghettos to the death camps began, peasants came with their carts and waited for the moment when they could start looting. Local gendarmes assisted the Germans in their bloody work of shooting Jews and helped the Gestapo to drag hidden Jews to the assembly places. Peasants caught them in hamlets and chased them to towns; sometimes they killed them on the spot. The Holocaust took place in full daylight and was witnessed by millions of Poles who—and this will be a very charitable interpretation—by and large did very little to interfere with it.

During the Nazi occupation, the Polish exile government in London and its underground organization were almost unanimous in viewing the country's future as a homogenous, Jewless state. Roman Knoll, a high officer of the exile government in London, warned in a memorandum sent from occupied Poland in August 1943: "the return of masses of Jews would be experienced by the population as . . . an invasion against which they would defend themselves, even with physical means" (Checinski 1982, 9). A week after the German attack on the Soviet Union, General Rowecki of the London-controlled Home Army, in a telegram, reported a pogrom in Brzest: "The population of the Eastern Borderland expresses spontaneous good will towards the Germans as deliverers from Bolshevik oppression, in which Jews played a large part" (Kersten 1991, 218).

Barely 100,000 Jews in Poland survived the German occupation (a year later some 250,000 returned from the Soviet Union where they found refuge during the war). Immediately after the war, pogroms flared up. Some 1,500 Jews were killed all over the country during the years 1945–1947 by Polish and Ukrainian anti-Communist armed bands and by the mob in more than a hundred towns and villages. They were murdered as "Soviet stooges," or simply because the survivors tried to recover their homes and belongings. The pogroms often started with medieval blood libel accusations.

The anti-Semitic upsurge was fueled by the presence of Jews in high positions among the Soviet-installed rulers, particularly in security organs. The U.S. ambassador Arthur Bliss Lane tolerantly explained in his report of July 15, 1946, the brutality of Jew-baiting by pointing to the "opposition of 80–90 percent of the Polish people against the government and especially the small but controlling group composed of Jews who have received their indoctrination in the Soviet Union" (Kersten 1991, 219).

The traditionally anti-Semitic position of the Catholic Church survived the occupation. When, in the city of Kielce, 250 survivors of the prewar 25,000 Jews returned to resume their life, a grenade was thrown into a prayer house. Cardinal Hlond expressed his "real sorrow" over the attack, but when the local Jewish committee asked the Bishop of Kielce to calm the population, he answered that Jews are good doctors and lawyers, but they should not meddle in politics and offend Polish national feelings. A few days later, a pogrom broke out, and 65 Jews were murdered. Cardinal Hlond found it again regrettable that Jews were losing their lives, but he put the blame on the victims by adding: "The fact that conditions are worsening should in large part be attributed to the Jews today occupying leading positions in the Polish government" (Kersten 1991, 218; Checinski 1982, 21).

Slovakia and Croatia

Let us round off this overview of autochthonous East-Central Holocaust with Slovakia and Croatia. Though about 25 percent of Slovak Jews were sent to their death by the Germans in the gas chambers of Auschwitz, with the eager collaboration of Prime Minister Monsignore Tiso, some 25,000 perished in the local concentration camps in the charge of the fascist Hlinka Guard. The Catholic Church gave its blessing to the destruction of the Jews. In its proclamation it declared in a time-honored East-Central manner: "The source of the tragedy of the Jewish people is the fact that they did not recognize the Messiah and prepared for Him a horrible death on the cross. They never altered in their hostility to Christianity" (Vago and Mosse 1974, 226).

Not less brutal was the regional character in Croatia. A quarter of the Jews were deported to Auschwitz, but nearly the total remainder was murdered in the twenty-seven local concentration camps. Here also the fascist state received the wholehearted support of the Catholic Church. Archbishop Saric of Sarajevo, a member of the ruling Ustasha Party, wrote loving odes to the Croatian "Führer" and compared him with Christ; a Franciscan priest, also a party member, became the commander of a concentration camp.

Let us mention again a revealing East-Central detail. According to a report in the *Los Angeles Times* (May 2, 1998), Dinko Sakic, commander of the two most notorious death camps, Jasenovac and

Stara Gradiska, ordered fifteen hundred arriving Jewish women and children to be packed into vans, fit rubber hoses from the exhaust to the interior, and drove them around the camp until the passengers were dead. His wife, a leading Ustasha functionary, used to go into the women's barrack of the camp at nights, point at one or the other inmate, and order the guards to strangle her with a wire. After the war, both Sakic and his wife escaped to Argentina, with Vatican help. Extradited from Argentina in 1999, they were tried in the "democratic" Cratia. Mrs. Sakic was acquitted of all charges; her husband's trial was "postponed" in view of his poor health.

On the German Holocaust

Fascist Germany occupies a special place in the regional division of Europe. In the fifteenth century, the German Reich, itself broken up in hundreds of small and medium principalities, was divided in two parts. The western and southern regions followed the West—even if the bloody repression of the Peasant War by the aristocracy for centuries prevented the breakthrough of liberal democracy. The foremost grain producing Electorate of Brandenburg with its ruling feudal Junker class, joined the East-Central region and introduced the Second Serfdom by forcibly expropriating and oppressing the formerly free peasants.

Under the House of Hohenzollern, tiny Brandenburg became the Prussian Kingdom. The Junker nobility was integrated into the military and the administration, and it had to serve the ruler with unquestioning fealty, discipline, and obedience. Prussia built the strongest army in medieval Europe and a powerful navy; it expanded the country to western (Silesian) and eastern (Polish) territories. The result was the "Sparta of the North," a militarized fusion of royal bureaucracy and landed Junker aristocracy.

In the eighteenth century, the enlightened absolutism of Frederic the Great paved the way for his successor to introduce in 1807 a "revolution from above," the first in the region. Royal edicts abolished serfdom, eliminated most feudal restrictions, emancipated Jews, and proclaimed the autonomy of the cities, but retained the military and political power of the ruling Junker class. The radical "revolution from above" as a gift to the quiescent people, predestined Prussia in 1871 to bring about the unity of Germany and open the way for a spectacular economic catch-up with the West. The country moved away from the East-Central region, but it did not yet join the Western one.

Belated national unity "from above" and the delayed start of capitalism determined Germany's future to a large extent. It widened the gap between rapid industrialization and a rigid Prussian sociopolitical system; it preserved an authoritarian, aggressively supremacist, militaristic ideology, without democratic tradition, without a progressive, liberal bourgeoisie. It also intensified the overheated and unstable nationalism of the latecomer who wanted to intrude in a world market already divided by others. It was this explosive mixture of reactionary East-Central Prussian legacy and advanced western-type industrialization that pushed Germany to unleash World War I.

The defeat was followed by a deep social, economic, and political disintegration and psychological shock. With the establishment of the Weimar Republic Germany politically joined the western region, but democracy was weak, as the Junker class kept its power in the army and the administration. The disruptions caused by the lost war and its humiliating consequences were soon followed by the especially devastating effects of the world economic crisis in an unstable, immature bourgeois society lacking any democratic tradition. All this contributed to create a unique constellation that led to the rise and triumph of German totalitarian fascism.

The attempt to explain the nature of anti-Semitism of Hitler-style fascism with such questionable entities as the national character or political culture of the German people does obscure and befog the comprehension of its horror and narrow down its irrationality to irrational formulas. The rise of German Nazi ideology can only be understood by the previously mentioned factors that paved its way to power. It offered a simple final solution to all problems: Exterminate the Jews, the instigators of all the misery in history, and the world would be whole again.

"The triumph of German anti-Semitism is by no means the result of the nature or character of a people which of itself, spontaneously showed perhaps less racial hatred than those civilized countries that expelled or exterminated their Jews already centuries ago," wrote T. Adorno and M. Horkheimer (in their preface to Massing 1959, vii). Though patently misleading for the period from the Crusades until the beginning of the nineteenth century, their statement is basically correct for the following 120 years. After the riots in 1819, virtually no pogroms occurred in Germany. The Jewish share in the economy and finance, and in the professions, culture, and science progressed rapidly; the only limitation of their full emancipation was their exclusion from the higher ranks in the army and in state administration; even this restriction ended in 1919. For the conservative-rightist parties in imperial Germany, anti-Semitic propaganda served mainly to gain votes in elections, and it was turned on and off according to its usefulness. When, in 1882, at the First International Anti-Semitic Congress in Dresden, a German delegate suggested the expulsion of the Jews from the country, Adolf Stoecker, the founder of a small anti-Semitic party, sadly replied that if ever the Germans would vote whether anti-Semites or Jews should be expelled, their choice would certainly fall to the former. Even the Jewish historian Simon Dubnow wrote: "After the consolidation of unification it seemed as if the Jewish question has been banned in Germany" (cited in Massing 1959, 3). As long as aggressive German nationalism was successful, the enemy was outside (the British, the French, the Slavs), while inside the emerging Marxist danger replaced the Jewish one. "Political anti-Semitism became superfluous. . . . The inferior race par excellence was not yet fixed," wrote sociologist Paul Massing (1949, 225).

For the Jews the Weimer Republic was a "Golden Age." Its fall was the beginning of their destruction. The full "exterminationist" character of the Nazi practice (but not of its theory) was an escalating process. Until the outbreak of the war, the authorities let 436,000 German and Austrian Jews emigrate, close to two-thirds of their total number. The only pogrom, the *Kristallnacht* in November 1938, was a pseudopogrom, organized from above and executed by the SA. It was not a sudden outburst of long-smoldering popular hate, but a methodically orchestrated "spontaneity," as Lucy Dawidowicz documents (1979, 136–41).

Emigration and pseudopogrom are indications that Hitler's "annihilationist" program had to be restrained because popular anti-

Semitism still lagged behind the propaganda. Even in the years of the spectacular rise in Nazi votes, from 2.5 percent in 1924 to over 37 percent in 1932, the 24 to 25 percent of the socialist vote remained steady, with acts of violence against Jews being sporadic. The party-led boycott of Jewish businesses, lawyers, and doctors got only a minimal response. Anti-Semitism "did not turn against 'the Jews,' but against 'the Jew,' a sinister-mysterious image. . . . It was the uniform opinion of every observer that except for fanatised SA men and their ilk, even convinced anti-Semites disapproved extremist measures as expulsion or extermination," wrote the eminent sociologist Eva Reichmann (1941, 280). The full essence of German fascism and its consequences became evident only after Hitler launched his war. The close connection of the Holocaust with the impasse and failure of the offensive against the Soviet Union are convincingly analyzed by Arno Mayer (1990, 279-408). On December 5, 1941, the "Blitzkrieg" was over, stopped before Moscow. One day later, the first death camp began to function, and one more day later, the Wannsee conference was prepared to outline the "final solution."

Under Nazi influence, the East-Central Holocaust was the culmination of a centuries-old inherent anti-Semitism. German fascism, however, was a radical break with the past, not an escalation of the "common" anti-Semitism of the middle and lower middle classes into genocide. Anti-Semitism was not just a political phenomenon as in the western region, not even a socioeconomic and political one as in East-Central Europe, but totalitarian in the strictest sense of the word, all-encompassing, even in a twisted way religious, with not Satan but with Jews in the center. Totalitarian anti-Semitism was, from the beginning, the essence of Nazi ideology. It contained the "final solution of the Jewish question" because it wanted to be the final solution for all the problems of the entire rejected modern history. Hitler could put into effect this nihilistic eschatology only by targeting a defenseless group. As early as 1919, he declared that in all movements in history that professed to serve mankind's own aspiration, power-hungry Jews were the driving force from behind. People were always the dupes, Jews the deceivers. At the very end, in the last sentence of his "political testament," he urged the Germans to "resist mercilessly the world poisoner of all people, the international Jewry" (von Brentano 1965, 63).

For German totalitarian fascism, the enemy had unlimited faces: communism, liberalism, democracy, Enlightenment, Catholicism, industrialism, war and pacifism, and behind all of them lurked the Jew. The non-Jewish, the postulated good world, did not exist any more because the Jews destroyed it, and does not yet exist because the Jews prevented its existence. A sick world needed a pathogenic agent, and it was Hitler's propagandistic cleverness to choose not an abstract bacillus like capitalism, but a concrete, clearly visible one, easily destroyable—the Jew.

Anti-Semitism became the official state religion. The consequence was the insignificance of personal, private Jew-hatred. The "ordinary" German, even a functionary of the system, did not need to be an anti-Semite in person; he was relieved of it. His private convictions were delegated to the state; he only had to demonstrate his outward consent if this was asked of him. To quote from a fascinating essay by Margherita von Brentano (1965, 67): "It was like with other state religions, you had to be seen in church, but it was not necessary also to pray. . . . Whether they were or were not anti-Semites, this was as unimportant as to ask a church tax collector if he believes in God."

We close this segment with another of von Brentano's astute formulations on the central meaning of the Holocaust for German totalitarian fascism:

The extermination of this helpless group of Jews was the preliminary for the planned enslavement and biological annihilation of powerful people. And as that did not succeed, it was on this group that it was substitutionally carried out. . . . The delusion of a world conspiracy of the subhumans could be made true on this powerless group by making them to subhumans and destroying them. (1965, 74ff.)

Hitler's fascism was not only a break with past anti-Semitism, but also with the traditional division of Europe in three regions. Germany's position had been ambiguous from the beginning. It started in the tenth century with a western structure, changed in the fifteenth with the secession of Prussia into an East-Central one, with unification became a hybrid mixture of western advanced capitalism and east-central reactionary semifeudalism, and returned to the West in 1919.

German totalitarian fascism broke the connection to the West. Politically, it destroyed democracy and installed a ruthless dictatorship. Its economy was dominated by the state and became fully militarized, a predatory *Grossraumwirtschaft* plundered and enslaved satellite and occupied countries; ideologically it rejected humanism, justice, the emancipation of mankind. For twelve years, the Thousand-Year Reich of German fascism formed its separate region, subjugated the western and the east-central regions, and part of the eastern region as well. Its chimeric totalitarian crusade ended with the Holocaust and with its own destruction.

7

People's Democracy: Theory and Practice

THE ATTEMPT TO BRIDGE EAST AND WEST

The East-Central European region collapsed with the war's end. The collapse was all-encompassing, human as well as material, sociopolitical as well as economic. Including the 4 million Holocaust victims of the region, about 9.5 million people perished, 10 percent of the total population. Estimates of 10 to 15 million people became displaced and had to begin their new lives in a new place, a new country, even a new continent. The material damages were estimated to be $40 billion in 1938 dollars. In Poland and in Yugoslavia, the two most devastated countries, the value of damages was nearly four times that of their total national income. Sociopolitical structures disintegrated: interwar ruling classes, political, and cultural elites, were decimated, killed, arrested, or deported first by Germans, then by Russian occupiers, murdered by fascist puppet regimes, or perished in civil wars and resistance movements. In the wake of the defeated German army, thousands of politicians, administrators, civil servants, and military and police forces, thoroughly compromised by their connections to the Nazis, fled to the West or were executed as war criminals.

In 1944–1945, the development of each country in the region took new turns, although variants of the same pattern, according to the different external and internal forces, and ended in 1948 in the uniformity of Stalinist communism. This intermediate pattern, called by the nebulous name "People's Democracy," is the subject of this chapter.

* * *

From the end of 1944 to the end of 1948, new specific structures emerged in five countries—Poland, Czechoslovakia, Hungary, Rumania, and Bulgaria. (Yugoslavia and its semisatellite Albania jumped over this period and proceeded from resistance to self-liberation to immediate Communist takeover.) The well-known antecedents reach back to Moscow. After 1939, during the first phase of the war, the Comintern repeated the old Leninist line about the imperialist character of the war, an interbourgeois affair from which the Soviet Union should keep out. Fascism was no longer the enemy as in the 1935–1939 Popular Front period, that role had been taken over by the bourgeois democracy and the Social Democrats. In June 1941, with Hitler's attack on the Soviet Union, the line suddenly changed. In the next few days, Dimitrov, general secretary of the Comintern, announced the new party line:

Proletarian dictatorship and socialism can not be on the agenda at this crucial stage of the world war. . . . Now we must have only one front, an anti-fascist front. He who assists the USSR in the war against Nazi Germany should be our ally, regardless of party affiliation, social background or social views. (Naimark and Gibianskii 1997, 42)

In mid-1944, when the offensive of the Red Army neared the borders of East-Central Europe, the political future of the region and the role of the Communist parties within it began to be reexamined. The result was the conception of the People's Democracy, vague enough to serve Stalin's double postwar goals, to secure Soviet influence on its borders, and still to be acceptable to the Western powers. Politically it meant a coalition government of democratic parties, whereby "democratic" implied "not anti-Soviet," economically a nonsocialist mixed system of state and private sectors, socially the elimination of past feudal and recent fascist structures. It stressed the necessity of following a path in accordance with the traditions and particular conditions of each country, an indeterminably long "third way" to an indetermined socialism.

What it was *not* was therefore spelled out, what it *was* was kept obscure—whether intentionally or because the initiators themselves did not know its exact character, is difficult to prove. Brzezinski cites some typically empty formulations from 1946: "A social order which differs from all hitherto known forms" (the Soviet economist E. Varga), or "Hybrid regimes combining features of proletarian and bourgeois democracy, but being in variance with both" (the Soviet philosopher I. P. Trainin). Not less clear are some regional formulations: "This specific order is not based on any existing model. It is not similar to the Soviet socialist order or to the economic system of the West" (President Bierut of Poland), and "We are following the line of national and democratic, not that of the socialist revolution" (Prime Minister Gottwald of Czechoslovakia), or "Bulgaria will not be a Soviet republic, but a People's Republic, in it there will be no dictatorship of any kind" (Dimitrov). Socialism was relegated to the distant future—Hungarian Polit Bureau member E. Gerö, an old Comintern executive, spoke of a "transition period of at least 10 to 15 years"—even if socialism remained the ultimate goal. "There is not only one road, the Soviet one, that leads to socialism. Each nation has to build its own road, taking into account the special conditions prevailing in the country. It has to be a Socialism born on Hungarian soil and adapted to Hungarian history," declared General Secretary Rákosi (Brzezinski 1981, 27ff.).

Was this lame "theory" a mere tactical ruse, or a sincere, insightful revision of the Leninist theory on the "inevitable dictatorship of the proletariat as the only road to socialism" in view of the changed international situations? The answer can be neither a yes nor a no. The maintenance of the wartime Great Alliance of the Soviet Union with the Western powers for a period as long as possible was of vital importance for Stalin. The Soviet casualties have been estimated at various times at 7, 11, or in the order of 20 or even 50 million. A quarter of prewar capital assets were destroyed, while the United States, the world's largest economic power, suffered relatively light casualties and no material damages.

Its economy grew during the war at the rate of 10 percent per year, not to mention its initial monopoly of the atomic bomb. Stalin needed a long breathing spell to recuperate. The Soviet Union could have imposed its variation of Stalinism on the occupied countries as early as 1945, but only at the price of an immediate rupture of the Great Alliance, and this Stalin was not ready to pay. His postwar instructions to the Communist parties in the region followed two simultaneous directions: it supported and strengthened their role in each country, but also restrained them to avoid any breaking point with the West.

To push this policy forward and apply the brake depended on three interlocking factors: the strategic considerations of the Soviet Union, the resistance of the Western powers, and the internal situation in the individual countries.

The strategic importance of friendly governments around the Soviet borders was accepted early on by the Western powers. Moreover, giving in to Russian preponderance in East-Central Europe gave the British a free hand in Greece and the Americans in Italy and France. The increasingly sharp conflicts, amply documented in the literature, revolved around the character of the coalition governments formed immediately after the war. The West demanded democratically elected coalitions. For the Soviet Union "democracy" meant dominance of the Communists and their fellow travelers, with the exclusion of some prewar "historical" parties it considered, mostly with good reason, anti-Soviet. The disputes ended with a compromise close to the Russian interpretation. The Hungarian provisional government was recognized by the Western Allies in 1945, as was the Polish government after including Mikolajczyk, leader of the Peasant Party, and at the beginning of 1946 they recognized the Soviet-installed Groza government in Rumania. The wrangling for a compromise lasted somewhat longer in Bulgaria, its Communist-dominated government refused, despite Western pressure and Soviet advice, to include Nikola Petkov, the leader of the oppositional Agrarian Party. In September 1947, Petkov was sentenced to death in a show trial. A week after his execution, the West recognized the Bulgarian government. The future of Yugoslavia always remained an academic issue for both sides. In 1943, Tito created a *fait accompli* by transforming his Communist-dominated Anti-Fascist Council of National Liberation into a provisional government, and two years later, neither the West nor the Soviet Union had any choice but to recognize it. Czechoslovakia caused no conflict in the alliance; the Beneš-led, London-based government in exile had been recognized in 1941 by the Soviet Union. A new coalition government, formed in 1945 in Moscow with a program written by the Communists and accepted by Beneš, did not raise any objections. The incorporation of the Baltic states into the USSR, for two centuries part of the Tsarist Empire, was not even seriously discussed.

The establishment of a cordon of Soviet-friendly states in East-Central Europe, a reversed version of the western-friendly *cordon sanitaire* after World War I to block Communist "contagion," became a fact even before the end of the war. The West chose to resign itself to the realistically unchangeable division of the continent, repugnant for them, but still preferable to the alternative of an atomic war.

After this very sketchy and selective outline of the external factors that paved the way for the People's Democracies in the Soviet sphere of interest, we have first to eliminate three countries from our analysis, before we turn to the proper focus of this chapter, the internal structures that shaped this system in East-Central Europe.

Tito's Yugoslavia, as we have mentioned, disregarded any transitory phase, his Partisan army liberated the country without any significant Soviet military help and proclaimed a Federal People's Republic with a sham "coalition" government in which eleven of the twenty-one cabinet members were Communists and the other ten safe fellow travelers. By the end of the war, Yugoslavia was in essence already a single-party Communist dictatorship modeled on Stalinist patterns.

We also have to omit Bulgaria. On September 4, 1944, the Red Army entered the country; five days later, the Communist-led Fatherland Front staged a coup and installed its own bogus coalition government. The relatively strong party had substantial roots in the interwar history, was respected as a leader in the resistance movement, and profited also from the deep pro-Russian sentiments of the people. The Communists withstood the lukewarm pressure of the Western powers as well as of the Soviet Union to broaden the coalition. Hardly two years after the coup, a fraudulent election gave the Fatherland Front an overwhelming majority and, with it, sealed the domination of the Communist Party.

Neither was Rumania granted any time to develop a genuine People's Democratic system. The population was strongly anti-Russian. The Communist Party, banned during the interwar years, was totally insignificant. It held only one post in the Soviet-installed first cabinet, led by General Sanatescu, and included a large number of high-ranking military officers, reflecting the paramount Soviet interest to involve the Rumanian army in the very last phase of the war. In February 1945, Sanatescu was replaced by General Radescu. After a bloody clash between the army and Communist demonstrators, the general delivered a broadcast in which he referred to the "Moscovite" party leaders Ana Pauler and Vasile Luca as "horrible hyenas, foreigners without God or country," no Soviet-friendly manifestation by any count. In a brutal ultimatum, the Soviet Union demanded the resignation of Radescu and the installation of a friendly government under the pro-Communist Petru Groza. In the new bogus coalition, not one single representative member of the opposition was included. The transition ended after only six months, and Rumania fell under total Soviet control. Here, as in Bulgaria and Yugoslavia, "People's Democracy" was dead even before it was born.

* * *

To examine the socioeconomic and political structure of People's Democracy, we have to restrict ourselves to three countries—Czechoslovakia, Hungary, and Poland—different variants of the same system. In the historiography of the region, the five postwar years have been interpreted mostly as a rupture with the past, the opening of a gate through which Stalinism entered and brutally wiped out the separate development of East-Central Europe. Retrospectively, this interpretation seemed to have been validated by the facts. Our contention is, however, that this phase was at the same time a continuation of trends manifest in the history of each of those countries, and an adaptation to the drastic changes in the international situation of the region. During the period of People's Democracy, East-Central Europe remained a separate region, but the balance of its characteristic mixture of western and eastern structures changed radically, as it did a hundred years before when, under outside influences, capitalism became dominant while feudal structures still remained significant. In 1944–1945, socialistic structures put their increasingly dominating stamp on development, but at the same time, it was utterly impossible to speculate either where this new, contradictory internal mixture would lead, even though the Communists conceived it as just a necessary preliminary to their ultimate goal of power seizure, or how long it would last. The answers to these questions was given by purely external factors, the outbreak of the cold war and the Soviet reaction to it.

Czechoslovakia is the clearest example of this continuity. In the interwar period, it was the only democratic country in East-Central Europe. The early industrialization of Moravia and Bohemia (as has been discussed in chapter 3) resulted in a mixed socioeconomic structure, with one foot, the Czech Lands, in the West, and the other, the mainly agricultural Slovakia, in East-Central Europe. In the united country, about a quarter of the votes had been cast for the two workers' parties, the Communists and the Social Democrats: even the third largest party, the Czech Democrats under Masaryk and Benes, tried to supplement its strong nationalism with a vague Marxism.

After the war, it became the only people's democratic country in the region free of Soviet occupation and with genuine democratic traditions. Due to its particular prewar circumstances, we have to put the concept of coalition and of reforms into a specific context and have to outline, in contrast to Hungary and Poland, much more closely internal political developments that led Czechoslovakia, without direct Soviet interventions, to the threshold of Communist dictatorship.

The continuity was especially personified by Beneš, as well as the trauma of the Munich Agreement in 1938 during his premiership, when the West had capitulated to Hitler and the Soviet Union had been the only country willing to come to its rescue. He headed the government-in-exile in London and became president of the reconstituted nation, the only country from which Americans as well as Russians withdrew their troops soon after the liberation.

The beginnings of the Czechoslovak People's Democracy reach back to Moscow in 1943, when Beneš discussed the future of the country with the Communist emigrant leadership. It resulted in an outline for change, a shift in the foreign policy orientation from the West to the Soviet Union as a guarantor against German aggression, political and socioeconomic reforms, and a "regulated democracy" with a National Front in its center from which fascist and anti-Russian parties were excluded and in which the Communists played a leading role.

This wartime outline formed, after the liberation, the basis of a specific Czechoslovak variant of People's Democracy, in many respects different from the Polish and Hungarian variants. The traditional democratic-leftist and pro-Russian ties determined the specific political character of its coalition. In contrast to Hungary and Poland, all the parties of the National Front put "socialism" in their program, though with different connotations. The Social Democrats used it unambiguously: "Our mission was not and is not to reform capitalism, but to abolish it" (Kaplan 1987, 34). The Czech socialist program advocated "the harmonious unity of nationalism, socialism and democracy," or as President Beneš formulated it: "a socialist democracy as a political, economic and social system, a new regulated democracy" (Kaplan 1987, 34). Even the program of the nonsocialist Catholic parties stressed socialism: "It is not possible to return to the capitalist system that prevailed before the war. The war meant the end of the capitalist era, we now stand at the threshold of a new economic and social order," declared the Czech People's Party (Kaplan 1987, 49). Its Slovak counterpart, the Democratic Party, recalled Masaryk, whose "socialist idealism, both scientific and intense, humane and warm, is now being realized with Russian help" (Kaplan 1987, 49).

Ironically, but faithful to the Moscow line, the Communist Party was the only one in 1945 that did not proclaim socialism as the order of the day. "In spite of the favorable situation, our goal is not soviets or socialization, but rather to carry out a really thorough democratic, national revolution," declared party chairman Klement Gottwald (Kaplan 1987, 50). The party even rejected nationalization in its initial program. Only on pressure from the Social Democrats and the trade unions did the government put in on its agenda, at the suggestion of President Beneš (Kaplan 1987, 35).

The structure of the National Front itself differed from the multiparty system in Poland or Hungary. Only the four Czech parties and their Slovak counterparts were included, the restoration of the rightist organizations of the old republic was forbidden, and the formation of any oppositional party made impossible. Even within the National Front, rejection of the general policy was punishable by exclusion and, with it, the loss of any political influence, so that the soon-emerging conflicts with the Communists ended, until the very end of the People's Democracy, with the capitulation of the opponents.

The peculiar structure of the National Front, combined with the socialistic program of all its parties, allowed much faster progress for the people's democratic reforms. Already in May 1945 well before Poland and Hungary, all banks, insurance companies, mines, metallurgical works, and large industrial enterprises were nationalized, about 60 percent of the industrial output became part of the state sector. In the next month, though lagging behind Poland and Hungary, land reform was enacted. Close to 3 million hectares of enemy-owned (German and Hungarian) land was confiscated and distributed to landless and poor peasants. A year later, in a supplementary reform, another quarter of a million hectares were divided. The reforms brought important changes in the agrarian structure of the country; about 80 percent of the total land became small or medium holdings, while the influence of the large estates was eliminated.

Nationalization and land reform changed the foundations of Czechoslovak society. The economic and political power of high finance was broken, the position of the bourgeoisie was weakened, and the state became the dominating economic force. While in the prewar country the peasants had been a conservative factor, in the People's Democracy they became allied to the Communists and the Social Democrats, the leading forces of land reform, and an important element in the eventual fall of the People's Democracy.

In May 1946, in the first and only free election, the Communist Party received in the Czech province 40.2 percent of the votes and 30.4 percent in Catholic, backward Slovakia. On a national level, 38 percent cast their votes for the Communists; together with the closely allied Social Democratic Party, they achieved a bare absolute majority of 51 percent.

The Communist success altered the political scene. While in the 1945 government, all the National Front parties had been represented in equal numbers, now Gottwald, the leader of the strongest party, was asked to form the new government. The pace of change accelerated. To the three pillars of the People's Democratic structure—coalition, agrarian reform, and nationalization—a fourth was added: the drawing up of a two-year economic plan that envisaged the further strengthening of the state sector and the start of industrialization in Slovakia. By mid-1947, the Communists began to force the disintegration of the system itself. They openly announced their new goal: the achievement of the absolute majority, though still short of the seizure of total power. The drive to strangle any opposition became more brutal; however, it remained formally within the democratic framework of the National Front. Step-by-step, they undermined and split their coalition partners, even their Social Democratic allies, infiltrated and seized the lead in the security services, trade unions, factory councils, and mass organizations and turned them into their tools.

After the start of the Cold War and the establishment of the Cominform, even this framework was set to be destroyed, together with the People's Democracy. We will deal with it in chapter 8.

* * *

In the cases of Hungary and Poland, People's Democracy is also linked to their past. The first postwar years were liberation *and* oppression at the same time, change *and* continuation of their history. They were a belated correction of the failed 1848 "revolution from above." The nineteenth century, as we have seen, opened the door to capitalism, but deformed it by retaining decisive feudal structures. The twentieth century brought national independence, but no democracy. The Horthy regime and the Pilsudski dictatorship excluded large portions of the population from any significant role in the political and economic life of the nation and prepared the ground for a semifascist way to catastrophe.

A series of economic, political, and social reforms with genuine democratic and socialistic features began to rectify the omissions of the past and found broad popular support. The most important among them was agrarian reform. In interwar Poland, the power of the landed classes permitted only slow and hesitant measures; they affected little more than 10 percent of the arable land. Only one-quarter of the large estates were divided, and about 20 percent of the total arable land remained in the hands of postfeudal land-owners. This long, drawn out minireform left the agrarian problem far from solved.

In interwar Hungary, there was no agrarian reform to speak of, and no change occurred in the ownership of land. Close to half of the land, the same as before, was in the hands of the big land owners. Almost alone in Europe, the country conserved its system of feudal-type large estates.

People's Democracy brought radical agrarian reforms in both countries. It fulfilled long-denied, centuries-old aspirations of the peasantry. The class of big land owners, a main factor in its social and political backwardness, ceased to exist. Poland completed the unfinished task of the past, all holdings over 100 hectares were divided. On the 14 million confiscated hectares, landless families got new land, and over half a million dwarf holdings gained additional parcels.

With the next important economic change, the first steps were taken toward state control and nationalization of the main banks and of heavy industry, combined with the start of a planned economy. This policy was a continuation of the prewar statist trends as shown in chapter 5, but it gave them a vaguely socialistic content. Confiscation of German capital and that of collaborators, as well as state control and nationalization of key economic positions were general demands, not only of the Communist and Social Democratic parties, but were also included in the initial programs of their peasant coalition partners. The war destruction and the ensuing economic chaos made strong state intervention inevitable. Contributing to this necessity was the reluctance of the Western powers to offer credits for reconstruction, and no significant help could be expected from the impoverished Soviet Union which, on the contrary, deepened the chaos by dismantling factories at will and, in the case of Hungary, demanded high restitution payments.

By the end of the People's Democracy period, factories in Poland with more than fifty workers were nationalized in important branches of the economy, which resulted in a state industrial sector employing 84 percent of the work force. All banks were taken over by the state, and foreign trade was put under government control. In Hungary, nationalization began with the coal mines and electrical power stations. The ten biggest banks followed; with it complete state monopoly of the credit system was achieved that linked important parts of the industry to a state sector already employing 58 percent of the workers. Both countries started a three-year plan with the central aim of reconstruction.

All those economic reforms had major sociopolitical consequences. Agrarian reform in Hungary, the most radical in the region, redistributed postfeudal estates and large peasant holdings among 650,000 peasant families, opening a new existence for about 2.5 million men, women, and children, close to a third of the total population. More than a third of the entire territory of Hungary was involved, and the whole countryside got a new agrarian structure of small and medium peasants.

While the extension of state intervention and beginning nationalization considerably weakened the economic and political clout of the industrial and financial elite, the land reforms eradicated the centuries-old stunting influence of the semifeudal social class. It deepened not only the influence of the Communists and Socialists on the workers, but created new allies in the peasantry and also gained the support of a significant part of the professional classes and intellectuals. As Z. Brzezinski, a leading architect of the Cold War policy of the United States, writes about the period:

These programs stressed reforms, political, social and economic, for which was great need. Indeed, enlightened public opinion could not oppose many of the measures recommended. . . . Much of the intelligentsia . . . had become alienated from the prewar governments because of their failure to cope with the existing ills. . . . A minority of them, drawn to Marxism, were willing to give their ideology a chance to build a better world.

The workers and industrial engineers, dependent on the economic recovery programs, were primarily interested in their factories going again. Rapid economic reconstruction was the most vital issue, even more so than politics. And to a majority of them, state planning appeared necessary and logical.

Politically active liberal elements in East Europe undertook at least partial collaboration with the Communists since it appeared that democratization went hand in hand with Communist reform programs. (1981, 6ff.)

Indeed, democratization ran parallel and connected to the modernization of the economy. In Hungary, as in Poland, liberation from German occupation freed at the same time large segments of the population from the thoroughly compromised postfeudal, antidemocratic, fascist regimes. Immediately after the expulsion of German troops, a process of "democracy from below" started, in many instances contrary to the intentions of the Communist Party. Local National Committees, composed on the pattern of the coalition government, replaced the old collapsed administration in villages, cities, and provinces. Land Distribution Committees initiated by the Communists were taken over by the landless and poor peasants who interpreted the legal guidelines according to their own interests. Workers' Councils occupied factories abandoned by their owners, took over the management, and with the help of engineers and technicians, set production moving again. Spontaneous work brigades sprang up to rebuild destroyed transportation systems. After the restoration of central power in Budapest and Warsaw, those populist mass movements from below were reined in from above.

What followed was, however, still a previously unknown democracy, though restricted, controlled, and deformed step-by-step by a coalition system that favored with its structure and with Soviet help the Communist-Socialist alliance.

In Hungary, the interwar peasant base and democratic traditions of the Smallholder Party helped it to achieve a majority of the votes in the free elections of 1945 and 1946. Even in 1947, after becoming a reservoir of all the antileftist forces, in a manipulated election it managed to keep this majority, together with oppositional parties outside the coalition.

Broad sectors of the population formerly excluded from any influence became shapers of the political life, part of the power structure and the government. A large measure of freedom of press, speech, and worship was maintained to the end of this period, though increasingly threatened by Communist gains in the power struggle between Right and Left that characterized these four years. The ideological influence of the Catholic Church, the biggest landlord in the old "noble society," was curtailed but not broken by the separation of church and state and the secularization of the school system.

In Poland, the unfolding of political democracy was considerably more restrained. The liberation from German occupation by the

Red Army was far less perceived as a genuine liberation, but rather, as a new occupation by Russia, the other historical enemy. The main anti-Nazi resistance movement had been controlled by the London-based government-in-exile, and factions of it continued the armed struggle for two years, now against the Russians.

The new provisional government was a bogus coalition dominated by communists and socialist fellow travelers. Only after strong Western pressure on the Soviet Union could the Peasant Party leader Mikolajczyk join it. For the Soviet Union, control over Poland was of paramount security interest, but pro-Soviet sympathies were restricted to the Polish Workers' Party (PPR— symptomatically, the only party in the region that avoided the "Communist" name). This psychological hurdle could only partly be offset by the gain of rich German territories achieved with Soviet help and by popular socioeconomic reforms. The government did not risk holding even a manipulated election until 1947.

All this does not mean that a democratization process of the backward postfeudal structures did not take place. For large segments of the population, the hitherto closed doors to participation in the political and social life became wide open. As the Polish historian Krystyna Kersten writes in the first inside look published in English on this period of her country:

Nothing could be more incorrect than to characterize society as a whole as rejecting the USSR, the Communists and their political power. The new authorities offered real benefits. . . . In each social group, whether peasants, workers or intelligentsia, social advancement beckoned and increased with time. . . . Workers advanced to leading positions, peasant youth had the chance to advance quickly. . . . The Communists and their allies did not merely publicize their platforms, they carried out, at least in part, the democratic slogans of the Left. (1991, 170)

M. K. Dziewanowski comes to similar conclusions:

These years were marked by transformations that had certain genuine democratic and socialistic features. . . . Certain latitude was allowed to non-Communist political and religious forces, provided they did not openly challenge the new order, the leadership of the PPR and the fundamental principle of Polish-Soviet friendship. The degree of freedom was not negligible. . . . In 1947, four freedoms still existed in Poland: freedom of worship, freedom of movement and choosing one's work, freedom to listen to radio, even to foreign broadcasts, and finally freedom of private criticism. (1976, 206ff.)

The process of democratization, restricted and controlled, was enhanced by the genuine belief of Gomulka, the general secretary of the PPR, in the principles of People's Democracy as postulated for the postwar period, in a Polish, not Soviet, way to socialism. On June 2, 1946, he declared: "We in Poland have established a road different from the Soviet one, without the need of the dictatorship of the proletariat, we established the possibility of a development similar to the parliamentary system" (Kersten 1991, 270). Exactly two years later, on June 2, 1948, the adherence to this road marked the beginning of his fall, and at the same time, the destruction of People's Democracy in Poland.

Within the socioeconomic framework of democratization and reform, the political struggle for the character of the development enfolded between those forces that opposed and those that pushed ahead with a socialist transformation. The former were concentrated in the peasant parties, the latter in the Communist/Socialist bloc and its fellow travelers. It was an uneven struggle in view of the eventual resignation to the inevitable by the Western powers and the active aid and pressure of the Soviet Union. It lies outside the scope of this book to follow the gradual brutalization of this struggle, it is described in detail in the vast literature published in the West and also recently in the former satellite countries.

While in free Czechoslovakia, the Communist advance was achieved mainly by inner factors discussed above, in occupied Poland and Hungary, it was decisive overt and covert Soviet intervention that stepped in every time, when necessary, and changed the balance in favor of the Communists. The democratic features, bourgeois or socialist alike, were gradually controlled, restricted, and distorted, to fit into the ups and downs of Soviet security interests, to follow the sharpening conflicts with the Western powers and, in the end phase, to get the green light, suddenly predated by the international situation, for total Communist control in all the countries in its sphere of interest.

8

The Destruction of People's Democracy

THE MARSHALL PLAN AND THE COMINFORM

The Cold War did not break out from one day to the next. The Great Alliance, formed by mutual interests to defeat Germany, changed in character after the victory, due to contrasting vital interests in the postwar world. At the wartime conferences, Churchill and Roosevelt accepted the preponderant security needs of a Soviet-friendly *cordon sanitaire*, but not the outright Sovietization of East-Central Europe. By 1947, as we have seen, the western-oriented coalition partners were decimated and forced into a desperate retreat, but in Czechoslovakia, they could still fight back. The Polish government was still headed by a Social Democrat and held fast to a non-Soviet road. In Hungary, the prime minister, as well as the president of the Republic, came from the Smallholder Party, and in the election, at the end of August, the Communist/Socialist left bloc achieved only 40 percent of the vote.

In Western Europe, however, the situation took a much more alarming turn for the United States. The Communists participated in the governments of France and Italy and gained significant influence. In France, they became the strongest party, and in Italy, together with the leftist Socialists, they polled the majority of the votes. Added to this was the chaotic economic and political situation in the devastated western occupation zones of Germany. It was much more this alarming internal situation in Western Europe than any threatening new developments in the politically subservient Soviet "buffer zone," where at that time Stalin was still anxious not to antagonize the United States, that prompted a radical policy change from Washington with the announcement of the Marshall Plan.

It was foreshadowed by the Truman Doctrine. In the spring of 1947, a historical about-face of U.S. policy began to replace the fruitless diplomatic wrangling with the Soviet Union by one-sided open military, economic, and political actions to contain Soviet gains in Europe. With the Soviet development of an atomic bomb, the possibility increased that Moscow's up-to-then defensive policy, limited to strengthening its given position, might turn into an offensive, expansionist one. On March 11, 1947, President Truman announced: "I believe that it must be the policy of the United States to support free people who are resisting attempted subjugation by armed minorities or by outside pressures" (Kersten 1991, 400). He then offered military assistance to Greece and Turkey respectively, against the Communist threat.

On June 5, the Marshall Plan was announced, an offer for economic assistance to Europe. It had the inseparable basic aims of halting a feared Communist advance into Western Europe, rebuilding a united western Germany and its economic potential, and forming a West European bloc. In the words of Undersecretary of State Dean Acheson: "As diplomacy and negotiations failed, we must use our economic power, in order to call an effective halt to the Soviet Union's expansion and infiltration, and to create a basis for political stability and economic well-being" (Yergin 1977, 308).

For the Soviet Union, the Marshall Plan meant an open threat of overwhelming U.S. economic potential, an attempt to use economic aid to undermine recently won, but still somewhat tenuous, Soviet gains in East-Central Europe. Its response, a few months later, was the establishment of the Communist Information Bureau (Cominform) to impose total Communist control over its security zone, the Stalinization of the region.

The origins of the Cold War have been debated hotly ever since its beginning. The most widespread view in Western historiography put the blame squarely on the Soviet Union, and it rejected the opposite view as "revisionist." The recently accessible Russian and East-Central European archival material, however, supports the "revisionists." The chronology is unequivocal; the opening shots in a long escalating and confrontational process were fired by the Americans with the Truman Doctrine and, above all, with the Marshall Plan. Though the Soviet Union and its client states were also invited to the Paris Conference on the Marshall Plan, the Americans, British, and French never intended to allow Moscow to be included. As Scott Parrish writes, citing an official U.S. archive document:

Both Bevin and Bidault [the British and French foreign ministers] assured the American ambassador in Paris, Jefferson Caffery, that the invitation was little more than window dressing to defuse domestic criticism from the Left. Both told Caffery that "they hope the Soviets will refuse to cooperate." (1997, 277)

On the other hand, Stalin, still anxious to maintain the Great Alliance, initially decided to send a delegation, headed by Molotov, to find out the details of the American offer and state the terms under which Soviet participation would be possible: instead of an all-European, country-by-country plan. When the Soviet proposal was rejected, Molotov stormed out of the conference and accused the Western powers of dividing Europe into two hostile camps. The Soviet rejection was followed, on the blunt order of Stalin, by all client states, initially eager to participate.

In the next couple of months, Soviet reaction was undecided; it vacillated between the hope that compromise was still possible and the acknowledgment of the final end of the Great Alliance, as various, sometimes contradictory, policy papers indicate, documented in the excellent work *The Cominform* (published in 1994 by the Feltrinelli Foundation in Milan, in collaboration with the Russian Center for the Study of Modern History, in Moscow, edited by G. Procacci et al.). In June 1947, Stalin proposed to Gomulka the initiation of a conference to set up an "information journal," not an organization, published jointly by several Communist parties. Only on August 15, 1947, did the Foreign Policy Department of the Soviet Communist Party draft a memorandum for the secretary of the Central Committee, A. Zhdanov, to establish an organization and change the agenda of the conference: "Fight against the attempts by the American imperialism to enslave the countries of Europe economically, discuss the relations between the Soviet Union and the Communist parties and coordinate their activities" (Procacci 1994, 4).

Zhdanov's draft for the conference changed considerably in the next few weeks; only the last corrections transformed it into the recognition that the division of the world in two camps must be considered definitive and that after the ousting of the French and Italian Communists from the government, there were no Western forces capable to reverse it—hence his severe criticism of those parties for their "non-Marxist theory of a peaceful transition on a distinct road to socialism, different from the Russian road," their "succumbing to the charms of parliamentary combinations" (Procacci 1994, 22).

The initial postwar Soviet directive of "national roads" was forgotten and repudiated. In the context of this book, we do not follow the international significance of this new policy line; rather, we restrict ourselves to the impact on the People's Democracies. At one time Zhdanov included, in his evolving draft, a severe criticism of the Czechoslovak Party which "did not utilize the presence of the Soviet Army and had not known how to take advantage of the favorable situation" to seize power (Procacci 1994, 20). The indictment was left out of the final text, as the condemnation of the Western parties was deemed enough to show the change to the bewildered parties of the People's Democracies.

And bewildered they were. At the first stage of the conference, September 22–24, 1947, Gomulka emphasized in his opening speech the informal nature of the meeting, reiterated the desire to rule out the creation of an international organization similar to the Comintern, and stressed the principle of a "national road." The speakers of all the other parties followed his lead and kept themselves to the originally proposed framework of a mere exchange of experiences. The sudden volte-face came in the second part of the conference, on September 25, when Zhdanov, to the total surprise of the delegates from the People's Democracies, issued new directives: No national roads any more but application of the Russian model: no mere consultations but coordination of the policies: no informal gathering, but strict organizational unity under Soviet leadership. While in the first phase, G. M. Malenkov, the Soviet delegate, still spoke of the "inevitability of peaceful existence between the two systems" and "friendly cooperation among peace-loving nations" (Procacci 1994, 89) in the second phase, Zhdanov presented the new doctrine of the formation of the two camps—the imperialist and the democratic camp—as a response to the Marshall Plan, the necessity to establish an organization for consultation and "voluntary" coordination of actions, thus legitimizing Moscow's right to dictate to the "fraternal parties" their domestic affairs.

The sudden change was accepted obediently and supported by the delegates. Only Gomulka tried to balk. During the break following Zhdanov's report, he convened the members of the Polish Politbureau and declared that he was opposed to the establishment of an international organization with supervisory powers of a foreign center, and he resigned as general secretary. Others also had their doubts, but those were quickly shed; Gomulka withdrew his resignation and, for the moment, put aside his objections.

The wavering and indecision of the Soviet leadership lasted from June 1947, when Stalin proposed to Gomulka the sponsoring of a "special information conference" to the first days of September, when Zhdanov submitted to Stalin the final text of his speech. While the proclamation of the Marshall Plan was the first shot in the cold war, the Zhdanov report, more than three months later, returned the fire and set into motion the subjugation of the Communist parties in the Soviet sphere of interest with the reincarnation of the Comintern and the enforced transformation of the People's Democracy in the East-Central European region into uniform Stalinist structures.

* * *

The details of the Communist power seizure lie outside the scope of this book. Under direct Soviet control, concentrated, coordinated attacks were started in all client states to destroy People's Democracy. The first to succumb was Czechoslovakia. On February 13, 1948, the Communists, in a veritable "Blitzkrieg," provoked a deep political crisis with their coalition partners, mobilized worker and peasant organizations to intimidate the opposition and forced the centrist—but not the Socialist—members of the government to resign. On February 19, the Soviet deputy foreign minister, V. Zorin, arrived in Prague and told his Czechoslovak counterpart, Jan Masaryk, that in view of the deteriorating world situation the Soviet Union expected from his country a greater loyalty and more support for Gottwald's efforts to solve the crisis. He was blunter with the chairman of the Socialists, Bohumil Lausman, warning him to side with Gottwald against the allies of "foreign reactionary forces," otherwise the Soviet Union might be forced to safeguard Czechoslovakia's independence. To Gottwald, he imparted Stalin's "advice" to take advantage of the crisis and stage a final confrontation, if necessary, with the help of the Soviet military. Gottwald refused the offer, saying that he was in full control of the situation and Soviet armed intervention would only complicate it domestically, as well as internationally. U.S. ambassador L. Steinhardt arrived in Prague, on the same day as Zorin, but could offer only the moral and diplomatic support of his country. In the following days, Gottwald announced the preparedness of the party cadres, the armed police, and the security services. He summoned emergency regiments to the capital and organized mass demonstrations all over the country. On February 25, Beneš saw no other alternative but to appoint a Communist-led government in "coalition" with leftist Socialists and some token pro-Communist fellow travelers. In twelve days, all the obstacles were removed to begin the Stalinization of Czechoslovakia.

The dismantling of the People's Democracy in Poland went much slower. In the severely manipulated and falsified election in January 1947, the Left bloc got 80 percent of the vote, and the Peasant Party, with 10 percent, became a marginal force. The next goal of the Communists was the final destruction of the Peasant Party and the fusion of the two working-class parties, the Communists and the Socialists. However, the goals still remained set within the concept of a "Polish way," to be achieved preferably by political, organizational, and ideological, not by administrative or police means. It has to be, as Gomulka called it, a "gentle revolution," limiting tensions and conflicts, corresponding to the concrete situation of the country.

The international situation changed with the announcement of the Marshall Plan and the establishment of the Cominform. At that time, Poland had already been written off by the United States. When Poland asked for grain and credit, the requests were denied because, as U.S. Ambassador S. Griffis said, "a dollar for Poland is a dollar for the Soviet Union" (Kersten 1991, 406). Moscow now pushed Poland to quicken the pace of transition. Growing pressure on the Peasant Party led to its rapid disintegration and forced Mikolajczyk in October 1947 to flee the country, fearing for his life. The pressure on the Socialists also intensified, but Gomulka rejected any forced absorption; the fusion could only be a voluntary unification.

In the eyes of Moscow, however, an independent Socialist Party was the last obstacle to be removed. With the Stalin-Tito conflict coming to a head, the elimination of an insubordinated Gomulka became an urgent task. The break came on June 3, 1948, following Gomulka's report to the Central Committee. In the context of our book, we reduce his speech to its main meaning, the defense of the "Polish road to socialism," of the independence of Poland, and the Polish Party. Neither do we want to detail the attacks of the Politbureau on Gomulka's "rightist, nationalist, revisionist deviations" or on his spirited defense, nor can we document the preceding Soviet directives given to Bierut, the Stalinist president of the Republic. It is known, however, that during parts of the attacks, Molotov was present. The conflict ended, for the time being, on August 22, 1948, with the removal of Gomulka as secretary general, and his replacement by Bierut.

With this, the Polish road to socialism reached a dead end. In September, seven right-wing Socialist leaders were arrested and charged with the attempted overthrow of the democratic system on instructions from a foreign intelligence service. In November, in a Stalinist show trial, they were sentenced to long prison terms. On December 15, 1948, in the starting atmosphere of terror, the delegates of the Socialist and the Communist parties passed a unanimous resolution for unification. The last hurdle toward Sovietization was crossed.

At the beginning of 1947, Hungary was the only People's Democracy where the rightist peasant, bourgeois, and clerical forces still commanded significant political power. On the eve of the Cominform meeting, the situation changed considerably. The Smallholder Party was broken up, its general secretary arrested, its prime minister forced to leave the country, and its votes dwindled from 57 to 15 percent. Purged of its right wing, it abandoned all hope of influencing the course of events. However, the Smallholders, together with the few splintered, disunited oppositional parties outside the coalition, still held a majority in the parliament, even if it was a powerless one.

After the Cominform meeting, the structures of the People's Democracy began to be dismantled and a Stalinist transformation of society was set in motion. In February 1948, a new economic policy postulated among others the nationalization or state control of financial, industrial, and mining enterprises still in private hands; the public ownership of all schools and with it the breaking of the influence of the Catholic Church on education; the enlargement of the cooperative sector and restriction of big "kulak" agricultural farmers, and changed the three-year plan in favor of heavy industry.

The political transformation to total political power proceeded at a fast and relatively smooth pace. The oppositional parties outside the coalition quickly disintegrated, their leaders fleeing to the West. The next decisive step to one-party rule was the absorption of the Social Democratic Party. Already in December 1947, it denounced its right wing; in January 1948, a mass desertion of membership to the Communist Party began; in February, the rightist leadership was forced to resign, many of them left the country with passports provided by the Communist minister of Interior. In March, a party congress under new leftist leadership decided to begin negotiations with the Communists to prepare for unification. In April, the fusion began for local level organizations, and on June 22, 1948, the congress of both parties declared the formation of a unified Hungarian Workers' Party.

The coordination imposed by Moscow is especially obvious in the destruction of the Social Democratic parties. It was replicated in the Stalinization process of all the satellite countries: Rumania on February 21, Czechoslovakia on June 27, Bulgaria on August 11, and Poland on December 15, 1948.

That left the problem of the Smallholders, but the party in effect liquidated itself. At a conference in October 1948, it accepted the principle of a socialist-type cooperative farming, acknowledged the leading role of the working class in building a socialist society, declared its support for the struggle against political Catholicism and the "reactionary Church," and even for the restraining of the "kulaks." Total surrender was completed with the resigning of Smallholder prime minister Dinnyés and of the president of the republic Tildy.

The closing step in this "year of change," as the general secretary of the Communist Party, M. Rákosi called it, was the arrest of Cardinal Mindszenty on December 23. With this, a 900-year-old social, political, and ideological pillar was swept out of the way. The Catholic Church had accompanied Hungary's history through western and east-central feudalism and capitalism, and even the People's Democratic period could only weaken it. Now it became constrained into the administrative-police straitjacket of Stalinism.

* * *

By the end of 1948, all the former People's Democracies were absorbed in the Soviet system. Dimitrov, who first formulated the concept in 1944, amended it four years later: "The Soviet and People's Democratic regimes are two forms of one and the same power, the proletarian dictatorship." The term itself became anachronistic, henceforth it was used only to cloak the Stalinist system in the mantle of democracy.

Stalinization broke the historical links of the incipient social and democratic achievements with the past. After four and a half centuries of autonomous life, the East-Central European region ceased to exist and was incorporated into the eastern region, now ruled by the Soviet Union. The historical dividing line which separated it from the West reverted back to where it had been set at the end of the Middle Ages.

9

The Stalinist Legacy

THE STRUCTURAL CHANGES IN THE DESTROYED REGION

The five Stalinist and the following thirty-five post-Stalinist years do not belong as part of the subject matter of this book, the history of the East-Central European region. While the short period of People's Democracy was a continuation and widening of this history, its modification and adaptation to dominant outside influences, as it had been happening so many times in the past centuries, the subsequent forty years were a radial break with this continuity. It was the autonomous region itself that became extinct and was forced to become an appendage of a basically different region.

We do not want to follow the development of its political subordination, nor to deal with the teroristic Communist dictatorship of the party-state with its bloody show trials, the structure of its command economy, and its militarization under the threat of World War III. After Stalin's death, the modified, partially reformed model of the same basic socioeconomic Stalinism could only be interrupted by soon suppressed moments of revolts in Warsaw, Budapest, and Prague, a glimmer of dashed hope during the interrelated "thaw" internationally, as well as internally.

What interests us is what legacy the collapsed Stalinist period left for the present and future, no more a separate in-between region, but on its way to be integrated into postindustrial Europe. It is with this aim that we outline the deep structural changes that geographical east-central Europe underwent in those forty years, the character of this first ruthless, then "soft" Stalinist-type modernization. The east-central countries, with their historically intermediate situation between East and West, tilting first to one, then to the other side, tried on a Stalinist basis to overcome centuries of backwardness and in just decades to catch up with the rest of Europe.

All the countries experienced the most rapid economic development in their history. While in the first three decades, the gross domestic product (GDP) of western Europe grew two and a half times, in the Soviet satellites the increase was four and a half fold. In 1938, the GDP of the five countries—Czechoslovakia, Hungary, Poland, Rumania, and Bulgaria—lagged 34 percent below the European average, but by 1973, this gap was reduced to a mere 20 percent. Formerly agrarian countries changed into industrial ones: the peasant population dropped in Czechoslavakia from 28 to 18 percent; in Hungary from 51 to 24 percent; in Poland from 65 to 38 percent; in Rumania from 78 to 55 percent; and in Bulgaria from 80 to 42 percent of the total. More than half of the GDP in East-Central Europe was produced by industry against a prewar third, and only one-third by agriculture.

While in the 1950s, forced industrialization and brutal collectivization crippled agriculture for two decades, in the post-Stalinist period stabilization and loosening, in Poland even abandonment, of the collectivization, the introduction of a partial market economy and increased investment led to rapid development. By the 1980s, the average per capital agricultural output reached nearly three-fourths, in Hungary, even 98 percent, of the U.S. level with the help of mechanization and the use of modern agrotechnology. As I. T. Berend, whose thoroughly documented work this segment closely follows, remarks:

A peripheral region that was unable to follow the path of Western industrialization in the nineteenth century, which saw its relative backwardness increase in the first half of the twentieth century, and which preserved its overwhelmingly agricultural character by the middle of that century, East-Central Europe now carried out a belated "industrial revolution." (1996, 191)

The economic transformation was complemented by social and cultural changes. War, Holocaust, and Stalinism destroyed the entire old high and most of the petit bourgeoisie, the political, administrative, and cultural elite. In rapid social mobility, their place was increasingly taken by workers and peasants, a "positive discrimination" pushed them into universities and the leading positions in the economic, administrative, and intellectual fields. The extremely labor-intensive industrialization and the collectivization of agriculture drove masses of former peasants into factory jobs in the cities and created a new working class from which the needs of the huge party-state bureaucracy was met.

The relatively poor societies became, to a great extent, homogenous as poverty was distributed more equally. In a system where nearly 100 percent of the people were employees of the state, an engineer or a young medical doctor earned only 20 to 40 percent more than an average worker. At the same time, expertise and excellence remained often unrecognized, and the general work morale sank to a low level.

Social reconstruction was closely linked to a genuine "cultural revolution." Education was radically enlarged and remained free on all levels until the last years. A preschool system was developed for children between three and six, involving most of the age group, while elementary schools offering basic education was lengthened to eight or ten years. The highly specialized secondary schools which, in the prewar period, had enrolled only up to 10 percent of the population, now encompassed up to 90 percent, even if only in a vocationally oriented direction. Colleges and universities accepted ten to fifteen times more students than previously.

The cultural field was heavily subsidized. Books, theaters, concerts, operas and exhibitions were made available to everyone. At the time of the collapse of communism, the population reached a much higher educational, cultural, and intellectual level than before the war.

Most significantly, a premature welfare state, encompassing all citizens, was built with a broad range of social services, even if on a qualitatively low level. Old age pensions, free medical provisions, child support payments, and long maternity leaves became self-evident. Heavily subsidized meals and nurseries were offered at many workplaces. Housing rents were kept extremely low. Vacation accommodations were granted to a major portion of the population at a nominal charge through the trade unions. In the "post"-Stalinist period, Hungary spent more than 15 percent of its GDP for social services—more than the United States and the Western European countries—and the other satellite countries lagged not far behind. Together with a constitutionally guaranteed right to work and the elimination of unemployment, a tight social net was developed, though in many cases of substandard quality, offering basic security to the overwhelming majority of the population.

By stressing all these economic and social changes and achievements, we do not want to mitigate the oppressive nature of the system: the first total then highly selective deprivation of freedoms and human rights for everybody except the ruling Communist elite; the growing, pervasive moral corruption; and the hermetical isolation from the West that began to be somewhat relaxed in the last few decades. As stated at the beginning of this chapter, our aim is not to analyze the Stalinist and post-Stalinist model, but to select some of the deep changes that Sovietization enforced after Stalin imposed a Communist version on the region and which necessarily influenced the present and future of East-Central Europe. We disregarded the political history of those forty years, the police state, and the national humiliation that drove Poland, Hungary, and Czechoslovakia to revolt, and the different ways each country took, within a narrow margin, the constraints that belonging to the Soviet bloc allowed. We do not follow the gradually relaxed dictatorship after Stalin's death in Hungary and Poland on one side, the little changed rigid Stalinism of the Rumanian "national communism" on the other, while Czechoslovakia after the "Prague Spring" and Bulgaria moved between those two extremes. The latitude was different in each satellite, but the limitations of it were set by the Soviet party and army, as well as by the virtually total Western acceptance of the status quo.

After 1973, the rapid economic growth gradually slowed, then stagnated, and finally declined. In the West, the invention of the computer started a new postindustrial, communication epoch. It transformed production and services, led to the introduction of robots and space technology, new materials, and energy sources. The Soviet Union and its satellites, with their turn-of-the-century technological base, already antiquated in East-Central Europe when it was built in the 1950s, were politically and ideologically unable to adjust and reorient their economic policies to these revolutionary changes. The economic crisis also became a political one. Again, to quote Berend:

As state socialism ruled the entire economy, the deepening economic crisis undermined the transitory legitimacy of the regime. Surplus income, redistributed by the state, disappeared with the vanishing economic growth. The moderate but increasing standard of living stopped entirely, the premature welfare state lost its basis, and the low-level security, including full employment, became uncertain. The emerging economic disaster gradually turned into a comprehensive crisis of the regime. (1996, 232)

The end came with the agony of the Soviet Union. Economically, politically, and ideologically, it proved unable to keep up with Western technology that also transformed the military balance. It lost its ability to control crisis-ridden east-central Europe and had to look on helplessly as Stalinism collapsed in the former region within a few weeks of November and December 1989.

10

Requiem for a Defunct Region

SOME CONCLUDING THOUGHTS ABOUT THE TRANSITION

The East-Central European region is no more; this specific historical entity ceased to exist in 1948–1949, incorporated into the Stalinist region. Forty years later, the collapse and disintegration of the Soviet Union and the Communist system released its satellites from subjugation, but the former East-Central region remained dead and was not reborn. Even its map broke apart at the first moment of freedom. East Germany was reunited with the Federal Republic, Yugoslavia split in to small hostile states, and Slovakia proclaimed its independence.

On the surface, the political change was promising in all the countries that regained their freedom. One-party dictatorship was quickly replaced by a multiparty parliamentary system, though fragmented from the beginning. In the developed center of the former region, the Hungarian, Polish, and Czechoslovak elections brought to power centrist and right-center parties led by the former underground democratic opposition. In the Balkans, in the backward, still mostly agrarian countries of Rumania and Bulgaria, as well as in the seceded Slovakia, ex-Communists with a changed name and a thin democratic veneer gained a majority of the votes.

Different election results also marked a crossroad for the future. The three developed countries were pulled to the West, and the backward Balkan states began their drift toward further chaotic decay; which of the two roads Slovakia will take is, as yet, undecided.

In all other respects, the initial transition from state property to privatization, from a planned to a neoliberal market economy was uniformly disastrous. High unemployment and inflation erupted, rapid pauperization of the vast majority, especially grinding among the elderly and the retired, on one side, and emergence of a thin layer, 5 to 10 percent, of *nouveau riches* on the other, opened a deep gulf between the few prosperous and the many poor, losers of the transition. A crime wave swept the entire former region, eroding public safety. The welfare system was gradually dismantled, and one gap after the other appeared in the elaborate safety net by which the state has alleviated burdens and pains of sickness and old age. For the social impact, it is enough to point to the average life expectancy. It had climbed, by the 1970s, to only 3 to 4 percent below the West European level, but has now dropped to where it had been about ten years before that.

Parallel to the social disintegration went severe economic decay. Even in the most advanced and best prepared countries, the first years of the transformation led to a sudden 20 to 30 percent decline in the gross national product, as industrial output fell by as much as 40 percent. In Hungary, rash destruction of the agricultural cooperative system combined with private plots, the only genuinely productive, prosperous sector, resulted in a drop of 50 percent in output, as well as in exports. In Bulgaria, reprivatization led to the slaughter of millions of sheep and pigs as the small new private farms could not maintain them.

Politically, the initial euphoria about the newly won freedom faded quickly in the deteriorating atmosphere of everyday life. In the fertile soil of lost security and unfulfilled hopes, the only "ideal" that reemerged was xenophobia and anti-Semitism. It is only the changed international background—Western democracies instead of German Nazism—that keeps attacks on Jews, Gypsies, and blacks sporadic and reins in mutual nationalistic-chauvinistic propaganda between Hungarians, Slovaks, Rumanians, Ukrainians, and other "alien" elements under a tenuous control.

We just indicated briefly the huge, complex problems that Central-East Europe faces. There is immense literature available regarding specifics of this predicament. In this last chapter, we try to ponder questions and answers, disappointments and hopes in the present and for the future. We focus our thoughts on the transition of the three developed countries—predominantly on Hungary, the birthplace of this author. We do it not only because it is the most promising process in shaping a united Europe, but because the future of the other three backward states is murky, depressing, and sadly remains, as so often in their history, a side issue on the international political chessboard.

Poland, the Czech Republic, and Hungary are pulled and pushed, with Western assistance and on Western terms, to adopt an open, fullfledged market economy and to dismantle the statist social structures, whether by shock therapy or by a more gradual variant of the same. The dire consequences are declared as an unfortunate but unavoidable price to pay for the transition.

By the mid-1990s, the dramatic decline stopped, the economy started to improve slightly, and runaway inflation was curbed. The governments released encouraging statistics about a turning of the tide and made optimistic prophecies about stabilization and future growth. However, the depressed general mood of the population did not improve, as the official indicators were neither felt nor trusted. A marked nostalgia for the past emerged in wide strata, by any means not for the Communist system that hardly anybody wanted to return, but for the lost security and predictability of life. It was a reaction to rampant crime and corruption among the new political and economic elite, to the stubborn persistence of high unemployment, and to miserable social security payments.

The dissatisfaction saw its political expression in the defeat of the center-right governments. In Poland, in 1993, and in Hungary in 1994, the Left, successors of the Communist parties, gained an electoral victory with a majority of the votes, only to lose it a few years later when it became evident that the leftists followed the same restrictive neoliberal policy as their predecessors and brought no tangible improvement to everyday life. A similar rejection of the center-right happened in the Czech Republic, in 1998, when the Social Democrats formed a government, but it will predictably be followed in the near future by the same disappointment and defeat.

Even a decade after the collapse of communism, a late 1998 poll in Hungary, the vaunted showcase for a successful transition, expressed the disillusioned mood of the population. To the question: "Do you live better, unchanged, or worse than ten years ago?" only 9 percent answered with *better*. At the same time, the defeated socialist prime minister Gyula Horn had to admit that the average living standard of Hungarians is still half that of Austrians, and a third of the population lives under the poverty level.

After forty years of communism, generations grew up with tightly prearranged and internalized rules and expectations. Initiatives and overambitions, nonconformist thoughts and ideas, any significant deviation from prescribed attitudes were suspicious and rather a dangerous hindrance than advantage to one's career or advancement. When the yearned-for free market society suddenly broke in, the forgotten capitalist state-of-mind had to be reinvented and the values of a free society relearned. The emergence within a short decade of a thin layer of entrepreneurs and professionals who "made it" is a considerable achievement, even if in contrast to the 9 percent, as in the case of Hungary, a multiple number tried and failed.

Under the prevailing impropicious circumstances of the transition, many young people successfully entered the industrial, financial, commercial, and service sectors. They established new firms and joint ventures with foreign investors, took over former state-owned ailing small and medium companies, and made them profitable, successfully exporting their high-quality products to Western markets.

In Hungary, the privatization of retail trade, shops, and restaurants is complete, and about 60 percent of the gross national product comes from private firms. It is a sign of progress, even despite its skewed balance: close to 80 percent of private businesses are engaged in trade and services, but less than a quarter in manufacturing. Furthermore, the great majority of the state-owned and subventioned big industrial complexes, the pride of the outdated Stalinist modernization effort, have not yet found a buyer; they practically still remain state property and, lacking state support, work at low capacity or are closed down, the workers unemployed.

With some variations, the picture of success and failure is similar in Poland and the Czech Republic. Mansions with swimming pools were built in and around Budapest, Warsaw, and Prague, and gave a new face to the cities. Cellular phones are ubiquitous in countries where millions of households have been without telephones or at least have had to wait long years to be connected to the network monopolized by the state. The old-fashioned author of this book, recently doing research in Budapest in one of the institutes affiliated with the Academy of Sciences, looked in vain for a typewriter; every one had been discarded and replaced by computers.

For the three leading countries, the direction of transition is clear: back to Western Europe. Their membership in NATO and their promised integration into the European Community do not leave any realistic alternatives. In the decades around 1900, after the countries regained their independence from the Austrian and Russian empires, there had been a half-turn to the West. However, as we have shown, the adopted western-type constitutions and institutions became perverted by regional structures. With the exception of Czechoslovakia, pseudoparliamentarism concealed authoritarian regimes, military dictatorships, and semifascist governments, easy prey for any overwhelming Nazi influence. Constitutional freedoms were subverted by manipulated elections, ethnic and religious hatred, and oppression. Now, after the Western victory in the Cold War, there is nothing left but a full turn to the West, a possible and, of course, desirable return.

At the close of the century, two interrelated questions remain: Were the catastrophic consequences of the transitional period indeed unavoidable? Or could the countries not have chosen a less painful road, in full accordance with the West and their respective governments? The overwhelming majority of economists and social scientists answer the first question with a "yes" and, necessarily, with a "no" to the second. Our answer, however, is much more ambiguous and hesitant.

Let us consider the overridingly decisive role of foreign assistance. For the West, winner of the Cold War, the future of the collapsed Soviet Union and its satellites was of eminent ideological and political importance. To avoid the predictable chaos and the unforeseeable dangers to world peace, the future had to be channeled into directions that safeguarded Western interests. The historically unprecedented task of transforming the Leninist-Stalinist economy into a capitalist free market society induced the West to reap quickly and fully the fruits of its victory in the Cold War. Leaders of the United States and of the European Community (EC) mobilized the Western financial world, the International Monetary Fund, the World Bank, the so-called Groups of 7 and 24, executives of the most advanced countries, to grant credits tied to strict conditions for the adoption of the "Reaganite" and "Thatcherite" model of neoliberalism, at the time the prevalent product of centuries-long western socioeconomic history. A swarm of specialists and pundits descended upon the ruins of the former Communist system, headed by a cabal of Harvard economists. They gave advice on how to destroy and privatize the statist structures, attract western private investors, and introduce a free market economy through total deregulation, without any state intervention, with "shock therapy" or a somewhat more gradual variant of the same.

Their advice, backed by similar tight conditions attached to the credits, were obediently followed by the new governments and the emerging new elite. They were joined by part of the old nomenclatura that suddenly forgot its Marxist past and became zealous neoliberals. They thought they could not do other than adopt the prescribed recipes, according to the Hungarian proverb: "It is the stronger dog that wins," in its much more vulgar original phrasing. Under the new unsettled circumstances, the collapsed economies were unable to produce sufficient internal capital accumulation. Central planning mechanisms were destroyed and relocated to Brussels and New York to draw up the concept, strategy, and framework of the transition. Any state interference was rejected as a violation of the market economy in its neoliberal interpretation. The theory of the vale of tears through which the East-Central region had to march to arrive at free market prosperity was readily accepted, not only by the central-right governments, but even more eagerly by their socialist–ex-Communist successors who tried to avoid any appearance of etatism, not to be accused of being the proverbial leopard that does not change its spots.

It soon turned out, however, that hopes were exaggerated, and Western assistance remained insufficient to lead to a neoliberal breakthrough. After a couple of years, when Western fears of political turmoil did not materialize, the enthusiastic initial pledges were drastically scaled down. Already by 1993, the average assistance for the collapsed region was a mere $30 pro capita, a fraction of the original promises, quite below the amount initially deemed to be necessary for the formidable task. West Germany, for instance, poured a yearly average of close to $6,000 pro capita into the former East Germany and still could not eliminate the deep social and psychological gap between the two countries.

Private foreign investments were quite substantial in numbers, but had relatively little impact on badly needed structural changes. Besides some impressive investments, for example, of American, Japanese, and German car manufacturers, or German and French telecommunication companies, most foreign participation was minimal. It touched only the surface of the backward basic structures and was mainly directed to real estate and retail trade, bringing easy and fast profit. Any stroll in central Budapest makes this trend highly visible. The best hotels, restaurants, clothing chains, candy and drug stores, quality markets and department stores were taken over by Americans, Germans, and Austrians. Huge new shopping centers were built, to cite just a few conspicuous examples, besides the often-cited McDonalds and Burger King. The streets are clogged with Mercedes, the shops filled with Western articles (from toothpaste, bottled water, and detergent to sophisticated appliances), giving the false impression of a society that enjoys import-oriented luxury consumption.

Still in the outskirts of the center and tourist quarters, the drab, shabby reality of the old system has hardly changed. Prematurely aged men and women carry their plastic shopping bags with simple food, squeeze themselves into crowded, ill-smelling buses to and from work, or hurry home after dark on deserted streets, scared of being robbed—and that is new!—into housing badly in need of repair.

We had little to say about the fate of Rumania and Bulgaria, seceding early on from the developed core, mainly because the exact outcome of their transition seems to be unpredictable. The present does not bode well. They have experienced mostly the dark sides of the collapse, and the emergence of market structures progress at a snail's pace. The International Monetary Fund and the World Bank show little interest in advancing their transition, neither do Western investors—the share of private investments in the Rumanian gross national product is about a tenth of 1 percent and even less in Bulgaria.

Neglected by the West, clinging to old failed structures, politically unreliable, they are left to sink into further sociopolitical decline, into a kind of pariah status. Their transition seems to lead rather to an even deeper relative backwardness. Their centuries-long history within the Ottoman Empire made them a periphery of the region, which they joined only in the late nineteenth century. Now they drift to be the periphery not of the western region, but of the European continent.

The future of the three center states, as part of Western Europe, can be in no doubt. It is not only in the interest of the West, but also the policy of all Polish, Czech, and Hungarian governments, as well as the wishes of their people. Ironically, it is the rightist, xenophobic, anti-Semitic, and nationalist fringe that opposes Western integration and looks for a nebulous "third way." Therein lurks a possible danger: the voters, disappointed with the prevailing uniform policy of their alternating centrist and leftist governments, might elevate the extreme Right into a decisive position and temporarily block the road toward democracy. The nucleus of this possibility already exists in Hungary, where the center-to-right governing coalition has to tolerate the support of the neofascist party of István Csurka, which recently made its way into the parliament.

While the final outcome is not in doubt, the question remains: Was, and is, all the burning pain and misery avoidable? In a general sense, it might have been inevitable. There has been no revolutionary transformation in history without victims. In the British case, it was the traditional peasantry; in the French instance, the nobility; in Lenin's Soviet revolution, it was all kinds of real and alleged "counterrevolutionaries" and "White bandits," not to mention the victims of later Stalinist terror. In the current east-central European revolutionary transition, casualties happened only in Rumania, where several thousand people were killed in December

1989, but in other countries the "velvet revolutions" victimized the majority "only" by taking from it the security of existence.

Specifically, however, the answer should be a "yes." The depth of the sacrifices asked from the people of the former region was neither necessary nor avoidable, had many mistakes not occurred. The roots lie in the narrow-minded ideological approach of the West, as well as the local managers of the transition. For both, only one road existed: The never-tried pure *laissez faire* capitalism without any protectionist policy and state ownership, a completely free market that eventually will solve every problem by itself.

The transition could not work without foreign assistance, but the problem was the character of this assistance. Western advice and tightly conditioned credits dismissed the argument that the market economy in the West looked back to a centuries-long developmental history, while East-Central Europe never had a genuine free market. They also disregarded the fact that the West itself does not follow its own advice; state interference with protective tariffs, direct subventions to ailing branches, import restrictions, quotas, and a host of other pragmatic measures are regularly employed to correct the allegedly self-correcting market. The state's role was especially pronounced during such critical economic times as the 1930s New Deal in the United States or the wave of nationalizations after the war destruction in France, England, Italy, and Austria.

Is not the social collapse in East-Central Europe a deep enough crisis to take a less ideological and more pragmatic approach, one that would have balanced Western interests with the internal necessities and conditions of the individual countries? Even the International Monetary Fund and the World Bank have begun to concede that mistakes were made.

The donors set the aid policy, but the consultants they sent to the premises translated it into specific advice. Their experience came mostly from work in South America or in Africa; they hardly knew anything about the state socialist structures they had to change and privatize, and they tended to give the same advice they handed out to Ecuador or Zimbabwe. Many were given lush living quarters, housekeepers, and drivers, and made exorbitant salaries. J. R. Wedel (1998) quotes a Czech aide official wondering, "just who is the intended beneficiary of foreign assistance?" She refers to the countless short-term consultants as the "Marriott Brigade," a nickname given by the Poles: the consultants stay at the luxurious Marriott Hotel in Warsaw, appear in the region for several days or weeks, are quick with words, promises, and good advice, then disappear. The Hungarians might call them the "Forum Brigade," the Czechs the "Intercontinental Brigade."

Wedel's criticism does not spare their bosses in New York, London, or Brussels, either. It is worthwhile to quote some other parts of her findings.

Had donors designed aid more thoughtfully and grasped the importance of taking into account the legacies of communism . . . they might have structured aid differently . . . Had they not sent such an ill-suited cast of characters, some of these legacies might have been overcome . . . If donors had treated the East less as if the blackboard of communism could be wiped clean, donor efforts might have achieved more of their stated goal. (1998, 185)

No wonder the initially unquestioned trust in foreign advisers gave way to disillusion. I quote again:

Today, as some Central Europeans match and even outdo their Western counterparts in extravagance and inattention to their neediest citizens, it is sometimes hard to remember the time when the excesses of the Marriott Brigade were universally perceived as offensive. This is not to say that all potential for antagonism toward 'the West' has disappeared . . . The lines of polarization are now primarily between those who have become wealthy with the collapse of communism and those who have not. (194)

Ideological blinds and blindfolds are also responsible for the mistakes made by the former region's governments. Let us look at the case of Hungary. It was by purely ideological considerations that the first post-Communist government destroyed most of the agricultural cooperatives, the only branch of the post-Stalinist economy that worked on a world-class level and brought prosperity to the peasantry. The consequences of the reprivatization were disastrous. The former owners were elderly peasants or their children or grandchildren who had not moved decades ago from the drastically shrunken agricultural sector to the towns and cities. Many of them quickly realized that they did not want to farm the small

plot and sold it or did not know how farm without the technological facilities the cooperatives had offered. Others did not have the
financial means to operate these plots, and state subsidies were
drastically cut—budget-restrictive, neoliberal policy allowed to
subsidize only 8 percent of the output value, against 40 to 45 percent in the West.

Production and export dropped to about one-half of its former
level. While the government accepted Western demands to slash
import tariffs, the European Community raised theirs to keep out
East-Central European grain. Hungarian export was possible only
by offering a low price that hardly covered production costs—
sometimes not at all.

We went into some detail regarding the catastrophic agricultural
transformation in Hungary to select a conspicuous example for an
ideological approach that disregarded social and economic consequences. The destruction of the farm cooperative was not necessary: They already contained many market structures and could
have been transformed into voluntary associations of free peasants,
following many similar Western models.

The uneconomic, unrealistic ideological approach vastly increased misery in the industrial sector, as well. It was unnecessary
to destroy from one day to the other an industrial structure, the
work of two generations. It would have been sufficient, and for
Western advisers certainly acceptable, not to dismantle state property until parallel evolved market-conforming production and legal
structures supplant it. Hasty privatization went hand in hand with
rampant corruption, nepotism, and criminalization, the latter in
both of its senses: Outright criminal elements paved their own way
into the emerging capitalist possibilities, and general tax fraud took
advantage of lax collection laws. Another Hungarian example: The
new head of the national tax office was involved in securing for
himself and his family lucrative positions in companies under the
name of nonexisting foreign owners.

While ignoring the huge, unprofitable, outdated Stalinist industrial complexes, multinational companies bought some of the few
state firms already well established in foreign markets, and found
roundabout ways to hide their profit by channeling it to their Western subsidiaries. Others bought up factories, then closed them in
order to eliminate a competitor.

Industrial privatization was a mixed blessing. On one side, it was a decisive part of the necessary and unavoidable structural change; on the other its overhasty neoliberal orthodoxy contributed unnecessarily to the pain of tens of thousands who suddenly found themselves unemployed. (It has to be added that layoffs were also a correction of hidden unemployment during the Communist era when a multiple number of workers and employees performed tasks for which fewer persons would have been sufficient.)

The lack of any domestic general strategy for transition, due to neoliberal blinds, is one of the main reasons why avoidably deep pain and misery accompanies East-Central change. No government policy exists for short-term, temporary measures of state interference, even if contrary to pure market philosophy, but indispensable to correct grave mistakes. There are no priorities set, no elaborate plans for investment, energy, industrial, or work force strategies.

The timid argument does not hold that, in this case, that Western credit would stop, that the European Community would not accept them. In Russia, the IMF and the World Bank squandered billions in credit for empty promises, theft, and destruction, and the only real transition was toward total chaos. For many years the West compromised, waiting and paying for illusory results of ideologically motivated conditions, in the mistaken belief that insider privatization, disintegration, and official corruption were only bumps in the road toward a free market economy and democracy.

* * *

The core countries of East-Central Europe now begin their unstoppable march back to rejoin the West in far worse condition than they were a 150 years ago when capitalism started to penetrate the region. Then, however, the half-turn to the West soon got bogged down and was reversed. Outside destructive influences and deformed domestic structures led to an anti-Western course and to ultimate extinction.

This time, the full turn is assured. Whether it occurs along a more or less painful road depends on the continued insistence on a discredited theory or the acceptance of its objectively necessary revision, taking into consideration not only the forty Sovietized years, but also the five centuries long separation from the West. The final question is only the quality of the outcome. A millennial history of East-Central Europe as a social periphery of the continent, of lost opportunities and shattered hopes, cannot be wiped out in a few decades. The core of the former region that rejoins the West it left five hundred years ago cannot undo the past with the fell swoop of shock therapy or its variants; exaggerated hopes and illusions will only lead to new disappointments. In the next century, Poland, Hungary, and the Czech Republic might still remain the backward periphery of the West, as they had been before their secession, during the first four hundred formative years of Europe.

The future is not very promising as the gap between Western and East-Central Europe is here to stay for a very long time. Any computation of the per capita gross national product (GNP) necessarily has to be approximative due to the different sources and different bases of comparison. However, we tried to put more or less valid figures to the backwardness gap, reflecting at least the trends in the two parts of Europe. In the period from 1860 to 1913, when the West was already on its way to industrialization, the East-Central region just began its painful transformation from centuries of Second Serfdom to capitalism: The GNP was 56 to 57 percent of the Western level and crawled to 60 percent in 1938. After the war, at the 1973 peak of the Stalinist forced industrialization and modernization of agriculture, GNP surged to 80 percent, only to fall back to 72 percent ten years later with the crisis in socioeconomic structures.

After the collapse of communism we have more exact figures from recent reports by the World Bank and the European Bank of Reconstruction (*Neue Zürcher Zeitung*, August 1, 1999). The per capita GNP in the former East-Central region stands now at 44 percent of Western countries. The average of the three foremost countries—the Czech Republic, Poland, and Hungary—reached just 50 percent at the turn toward the twenty-first century, lower than a hundred years ago.

More alarming is the pyschological perception of this gap. In a 1999 poll taken by the Hungarian Institute of Social Research a somewhat questionable 80 percent of the interviewees declared that their standard of living was lower than it has been in 1989. Not much different, but from another angle, is the central European poll by the Institute of Consumer Research in Vienna: 23 percent of Hungarians are satisfied with the present system, 66 percent are disappointed, 11 percent said that they did not expect any change for the better, therefore they cannot be disappointed (*Vasárnapi Hirek*, August 8, 1999).

Alarming results, but they might contain a glimmer of hope also. Young and old still remember that there was a time when everybody's existence seemed to be secure. There were no beggars, no homeless, no unemployed, and the basic necessities of life were provided within one's means by the "paternalistic" state. True, it was a very low-level, low-quality security, bought at the price of political oppression, ideological lies, and restricted personal freedom. But the young knew that after finishing school a job would be waiting; for the old, living on miserable social security payments, destitution seemed more bearable in view of the general poverty around them; and the emerging middle class was happy to find a somewhat better life in the nooks and cracks of a "softened" dictatorship. Now, the constraints of the past have faded away against the pain of lost security. This is at the root of the persistent nostalgia for the collapsed regime.

Perhaps for future generations of the former region the memory will stay alive, and a belief will emerge that existential security is not a utopia, not a communist experiment doomed to failure. It could be a new chapter in the constantly changing democratic development of the region. The current neoliberal faith is not the end of history.

Bibliography

Anderson, P. *Passages from Antiquity to Feudalism.* London: NLB, 1978.

Barraclough, G. *Eastern and Western Europe During the Middle Ages.* London: Thames and Hudson, 1970.

Bell, J. D. *The Bulgarian Communist Party.* Stanford, Calif.: Hoover Institution Press, 1986.

Berend, I. T. *Decades of Crisis: Central and Eastern Europe Before World War II.* Berkeley: University of California Press, 1998.

———. *Central and Eastern Europe, 1944–1993.* New York: Cambridge University Press, 1996.

Berend, I. T., and G. Ranki. *The European Periphery and Industrialization.* New York: Cambridge University Press, 1954.

———. *Economic Development in East Central Europe in the 19th and 20th Centuries.* New York: Columbia University Press, 1974.

Blum, J. *Lord and Peasant in Russia.* Princeton, N.J.: Princeton University Press, 1961.

von Bretano, M. "Die Endlösung." (The Final Solution). In *Antisemitismus,* edited by H. Huss and A. Schröder. Frankfurt/Main: Europäische Verlagsanstalt, 1965.

Brown, J. F. *Eastern Europe and Communist Rule.* Durham, N.C.: Duke University Press, 1988.

Brzezinski, Z. *The Soviet Bloc: Unity and Conflict.* Cambridge, Mass.: Harvard University Press, 1981.

Buttnaru, I. C. *The Silent Holocaust: Rumania and its Jews.* New York: Greenwood Press, 1992.

Carsten, F. L. *The Origins of Prussia.* Oxford: Clavendon Press, 1954.

Checinski, M. *Poland: Communism, Nationalism, Antisemitism.* New York: Karz-Cohl, 1982.

Chirot, D. *Social Change in a Peripherial Society.* New York: Academy Press, 1976.

————, ed. *The Origins of Backwardness in Eastern Europe.* University of California Press, 1989.

Dawidowicz, L. *The War Against the Jews, 1933–1945.* New York: Penguin, 1979.

Deak, I. "Hungary." In *The European Right,* edited by H. Rogger and E. Weber. Berkeley: University of California Press, 1966.

————. *The Lawful Revolution: Louis Kossuth and the Hungarians.* New York: Columbia University Press, 1979.

Dobb, M. *Studies in the Development of Capitalism.* New York: International Publishers, 1963.

Dubnow, Simon. *The Recent History of the Jewish People.* Vol. 3. N.P.: Jerusalem, 1935 (in German).

Dziewanowski, M. K. *The Communist Party of Poland.* Cambridge, Mass.: Harvard University Press, 1976.

Endres, A. *Revolution in Österreich 1848.* Vienna Danubia Verlag, 1947.

Fejtö, F. *Histoire des démocraties populaires.* Paris: Editions du Seuil, 1952.

Fleming, D. F. *The Cold War and Its Origins, 1917–1960.* New York: Doubleday, 1961.

Florinsky, M. T. *Russia: A History and an Interpretation.* New York: Macmillan, 1953.

Fontaine, A. *A History of the Cold War.* New York: Pantheon Books, 1969.

Gati, C. *Hungary and the Soviet Bloc.* Durham N.C.: Duke University Press, 1985.

————. *The Bloc that Failed.* Bloomington: Indiana University Press, 1990.

Gerschenkron, A. *Economic Backwardness in Historical Perspective.* Cambridge, Mass.: Belknap Press of Harvard University Press, 1962.

Gibianskii, L. "The Soviet-Yugoslav Split and the Cominform." In *The Establishment of Communist Regimes in Eastern Europe 1944–*

1949, edited by N. Naimark and L. Gibianskii. Boulder, Colo.: Westview Press, 1997.

Heller, C. S. *On the Edge of Destruction: Jews of Poland between the Two World Wars*. New York: Columbia University Press, 1977.

Hobsbawm, E. *The Age of Revolution, 1789–1848*. New York: Praeger, 1969.

———. *The Age of Capital, 1848–1875*. New York: Scribnors, 1975.

———. *The Age of Empire, 1875–1914*. New York: Pantheon, 1987.

———. *The Age of Extremes, 1914–1991*. New York: Pantheon, 1994.

Horowitz, D. *The Free World Colossus: Critique of the American Policy in the Cold War*. New York: Hill and Wang, 1977.

Ionescu, G. *Communism in Rumania, 1944–1962*. Westport, Conn.: Greenwood Press, 1976.

Janos, A. C. *The Politics of Backwardness in Hungary*. Princeton, N.J.: Princeton University Press, 1982.

Jaszi, O. *The Dissolution of the Habsburg Monarchy*. Chicago: University of Chicago Press, 1961.

Jones, J. R. "England." In *The European Right*, edited by H. Rogger and E. Weber. Berkeley: University of California Press, 1966.

Jowitt, K., ed. *Social Change in Rumania, 1860–1940*. Berkeley: University of California Press, 1978.

Kaplan, K. *The Short March: The Communist Takeover in Czechoslovakia, 1945–1948*. New York: St. Martin's Press, 1987.

Kaser, M. S. and E. A. Radice. *The Economic History of Eastern Europe, 1919–1975*. New York: Oxford University Press, 1985.

Kersten, K. *The Establishment of Communist Rule in Poland, 1943–1948*. Berkeley: University of California Press, 1991.

Kochan, L. *The Making of Modern Russia*. London: Penguin, 1997.

Kornai, J. *The Socialist System: The Political Economy of Communism*. Princeton, N.J.: Princeton University Press, 1992.

Kovrig, B. *Communism in Hungary: From Kun to Kádár*. Stanford, Calif.: Hoover Institution Press, 1979.

Lévai, J. *Zsidó sors Magyarországon*. (Jewish doom in Hungary). Budapest: Magyar Téka, 1948.

McCagg, W. O., Jr. *A History of Habsburg Jews, 1670–1918*. Bloomington: Indiana University Press, 1989.

McCauley, M., ed. *Communist Power in Europe, 1944–1949*. New York: Harper & Row, 1977.

Massing, P. *Vorgeschichte des politischen Antisemitismus*. Frankfurt/Main: Europäische Verlagsanstalt, 1959. Original American edition, *Rehearsal for Destruction*. New York: Harper, 1949.

Mastny, V. *The Cold War and Soviet Insecurity: The Stalin Years*. New York: Oxford University Press, 1996.

Mayer, A. J. *Why Did the Heavens Not Darken? The Final Solution in History*. New York: Pantheon, 1990.

Moore, B., Jr. *Social Origins of Dictatorship and Democracy*. Boston: Beacon Press, 1967.

Naimark, N., and L. Gibianskii, eds. *The Establishment of Communist Regimes in Eastern Europe, 1944–1949*. Boulder, Colo.: Westview Press, 1997.

Parrish, S. "The Marshall Plan, Soviet-American Relations and the Division of Europe." In *The Establishment of Communist Regimes in Eastern Europe, 1944–1949*, edited by N. Naimark and L. Gibianskii. Boulder, Colo.: Westview Press, 1997.

Poliakov, L. *The History of Anti-Semitism: From the Time of Christ to the Court Jews*. New York: Schocken, 1974.

Procacci, G., et al., eds. *The Cominform: Minutes of the Three Conferences 1947/1948/1949*. Milan: Fondazione Feltrinelli, 1994.

Reddaway, W. M., and H. Parson, eds. *The Cambridge History of Poland*. Cambridge, Eng.: Cambridge University Press, 1950.

Reichmann, E. *Flucht in den Hass*. Frankfurt/Main: Europäische Verlagsanstalt, 1949. Original English edition, *Hostages of Civilisation*. London: Gollancz, 1941.

Roberts, H. *Rumania: Political Problems of an Agrarian State*. New Haven, Conn.: Yale University Press, 1951.

Rogger, H., and E. Weber, eds. *The European Right*. Berkeley University of California Press, 1966.

Rothschild, J. *East Central Europe between the Two World Wars*. Seattle: University of Washington Press, 1974.

Spulber, N. *The State and Economic Development in Eastern Europe*. New York: Random House, 1966.

Stengers, G. "Belgium." In *The European Right*, edited by H. Rogger and E. Weber. Berkeley: University of California Press, 1966.

Stokes, G. "The Social Origins of Eastern European Politics." In *The Origins of Backwardness in Eastern Europe*, edited by D. Chirot. Berkeley: University of California Press, 1989.

Sugar, P. S. *Southeastern Europe under Ottoman Rule*. Seattle: University of Washington Press, 1977.

Szücs, J. *The Three Historical Regions of Europe*. Budapest: Academy Publisher, 1983.

Taubman, W. *Stalin's American Policy: From Entente to Detante to Cold War*. New York: Norton, 1982.

Taylor, J. *The Economic Development of Poland, 1919–1950*. Ithaca, N.Y.: Cornell University Press, 1952.

Thomas, H. *Armed Truce: The Beginnings of the Cold War*. New York: Atheneum, 1987.

Thompson, J. M. *Russia and the Soviet Union*. Boulder, Colo.: Westview Press, 1998.

Ulam, A. B. *Titoism and the Cominform*. Westport, Conn.: Greenwood Press, 1952.

Vago, B., and G. Mosse, eds. *Jews and Non-Jews in Eastern Europe, 1918–1948*. New York: Wiley, 1974.

Wandycz, P. S. *The Lands of Partitioned Poland, 1795–1918*. Seattle: University of Washington Press, 1974.

Weber, E. "France." In *The European Right*, edited by H. Rogger and E. Weber. Berkeley: University of California Press, 1966.

———. "Romania." In *The European Right*, edited by H. Rogger and E. Weber. Berkeley: University of California Press, 1966.

Wedel, Janine R. *Collision and Collusion: The Strange Case of Western Aid to Eastern Europe, 1989–1998*. New York: St. Martin's Press, 1998.

Wolff, R. L. *The Balkans in Our Time*. New York: Norton, 1978.

Woolfe, S. J. *Fascism in Europe*. London: Methuen, 1981.

Yergin, D. *Shattered Peace: The Origins of the Cold War and the National Security State*. Boston: Houghton Mifflin, 1977.

Zubok, A., and C. Plechakov. *Inside the Kremlin's Cold War*. Cambridge, Mass.: Harvard University Press, 1996.

Index

Galicia: abolition of serfdom, 33;
agrarian colony of the Empire,
31; anti-Semitism, 76–77;
averted revolution, uprising in
Krakow, 36; part of the Habsburg Empire, leading role of Polish aristocracy, 30
German anti-Semitism and the
Holocaust: historical background, 94–95; Jews in
pre-Hitler Germany, 95–97; totalitarian character of the Holocaust, 97–99
Germany, 24–25, 94–99
Gerö, Ernö, 103
Gomulka, Wladislaw: fall of, 123;
opposition to Soviet model, 64,
121; Polish way to socialism,
115. See also Cominform; People's Democracy; Poland
Gottwald, Klement, 103, 110, 122
Great Alliance: break-up of, 117–
21; continuation of the anti-
Hitler coalition and conflicting
interests, 104–05. See also Cominform; Marshall Plan; Truman
Doctrine
Groza, Petru, 104, 106

Habsburg Empire, 25; fragile
unity and centralization, half-
western structures, 29–31; inte-
grating frame of Central
Europe, 29. See also individual
countries
Hlinka Guard, 93
Hlond, August, 79–80
Holocaust: in East-Central Europe,
87–94; in the West, 74–75. See
also individual countries
Horn, Gyula, 136
Horthy, Miklós, 110

Hungary: agrarian colony of the
Empire, 31; compromise between the Habsburg Dynasty
and the feudal nation, 29–30;
defeat by Turkish army and division of the country, 28–29;
foreign capital, 52–56; German
penetration and war economy,
66–67; Holocaust, 89–91; Jewish and German bourgeoisie, 38;
political radicalization and
Communist power seizure, 124–
25; reforms and party struggles,
110–13; revolution of 1848–49,
33–35; rise of fascism, 80–83;
under Stalinism, 128 and passim;
state intervention, 64–66; unchanged rule of nobility, agrarian backwardness, 37–38; as a
variant of People's Democracy,
106; Western feudal structure
and peasant war, 26–27
Hussite movement, 25

Industrial Revolution, in England,
7
Industry and banking in: Austria,
37; the Balkan countries, 53–54,
61–64; Bohemia, 30–31, 39–40;
Bulgaria, 68–69; Hungary, 39,
53, 58, 65–67; Poland, 59–60;
Rumania, 47, 53, 56, 58, 60–
61, 67–68; under Stalinism, 128
and passim
Ivan III, 5

Jews in: Galicia, 76–77; Hungary,
38, 80–83; Poland, 77–80; Rumania, 47, 59, 61, 85–87; Wala-
chia/Moldavia, 84–85; the West,
72–74. See also Holocaust
Jókai, Mór, 34

156 • Index

About the Author

GEORGE H. HODOS has taught East European history at the University of Vienna and is Scientific Advisor of the *Yearbook of Historical Research about Communism* at the University of Mannheim in Germany. Born in 1921 in Hungary, Hodos immigrated in 1939 to Switzerland where he studied at the University of Zurich and joined the Communist Party. After the war he returned to Hungary as an editor of economic journals and a correspondent for Western newspapers. In 1949 he was arrested, convicted in a show trial as an "American spy," and, after Stalin's death, rehabilitated. He immigrated to the United States via Austria after the Hungarian revolution of 1956.

ISBN 0-275-95497-8

9 780275 954970

HARDCOVER BAR CODE